THE WELSH REVIVAL OF 1904

MAP OF WALES
showing counties and
centres mentioned

THE WELSH REVIVAL OF 1904

EIFION EVANS

Foreword by
D. MARTYN LLOYD-JONES

EVANGELICAL PRESS OF WALES

© EVANGELICAL MOVEMENT OF WALES, 1969

FIRST PUBLISHED 1969
PAPERBACK EDITION 1974
REPRINTED 1981, 1984
THIRD EDITION (WITH INDEX) 1987
REPRINTED 1989

ISBN 1 85049 037 6

(First Edition — ISBN 0 900898 03 8)
(Second Edition — ISBN 0 900898 59 3)

Cover photograph:
Cockle-picking at dawn on the estuary near Loughor, the home of
Evan Roberts (by courtesy of the Wales Tourist Board).

PUBLISHED BY THE EVANGELICAL PRESS OF WALES
BRYNTIRION, BRIDGEND, MID GLAMORGAN CF31 4DX, WALES

PRINTED BY BILLING & SONS LIMITED, WORCESTER WR2 5JU

FOREWORD

I am very happy indeed to write this Foreword to, and to recommend, this study of the Welsh Revival of 1904-5.

This is something which has been badly needed for years, and should be of especial value to people like myself, who were too young to remember the revival itself, but who have known those who had been prominent in the revival and the many who had benefited by it.

I am particularly pleased by the way in which this study has been written; for it is not a mere recital of facts, but truly a study. This is good because certain features of the revival had always posed problems—theological and psychological.

Dr. Eifion Evans has dealt with all this in a thoroughly satisfactory manner, indeed, in a unique manner. What was needed was a writer who was a trained historian, able to take an objective view, and yet at the same time one who was able to deal with the subject theologically. Moreover, it called for a writer with spiritual insight, understanding, and sympathy. Dr. Evans combines these qualities in an exceptional way with a result that his book is invaluable, not only as a study of this particular revival, but also as a study of the phenomenon of revival in general.

This is particularly important at the present time for the following reasons:

First, the great need of revival in the churches. This is surely the only real hope; but it is essential that Christians should be clear as to the difference between revival and organized evangelism. Here is a reminder of what is possible, and especially for those whose whole doctrine of the Holy Spirit really leaves no room for revival.

Secondly, this book is most opportune because of what is known as the "Charismatic Movement" and a new interest in spiritual phenomena. It helps to show the danger of passing from the spiritual to the psychological and possibly even the psychic.

There are undoubtedly many problems in connection with the Revival of 1904-5—certain tendencies to extreme mysticism in Mr. Evan Roberts himself, the general difference in character between this revival and previous revivals, and the lamentable failure of the preachers to continue preaching and teaching during the revival, etc. All these are dealt with in a most judicious manner by Dr. Evans. All revivals have produced problems—life always does so—and the danger is to dismiss the entire phenomenon because of certain excesses that often accompany it.

No one can read this book without coming under judgement. It will reveal whether our ultimate faith is in "the power of God" or in human ability and organizations. It is my prayer, and my hope, that it will lead many so to realize anew and afresh the glory and the wonder of the former that they will begin to long and to yearn and to pray for another "visitation from on high" such as was experienced in 1904-5.

June, 1969.   D. M. LLOYD-JONES.

CONTENTS

ACKNOWLEDGMENTS

Many friends have graciously prompted me to write this book. Chief among these is the Rev. James H. Walters, B.A., minister of Moriah, Loughor, the church to which Evan Roberts belonged and where some of the most powerful influences of the revival were felt. I am deeply grateful for his faithful and sustained interest in the work, and for my wife's encouragement over the period of its preparation.

Dr. J. Edwin Orr of Los Angeles has also stimulated perseverance by virtue of his own interest in revivals and especially as he was writing a survey of world-wide awakenings in the early twentieth century. I am indebted to him for access to his fully-documented accounts.

No study of this kind would be possible without assistance in tracing manuscripts and books, and for such help I am thankful to Miss K. Monica Davies, M.A., F.L.A., of the National Library of Wales.

To Mrs. Margaret Hull I owe a special debt of gratitude for so patiently and accurately transforming an almost illegible manuscript into a typewritten copy.

Dr. D. Martyn Lloyd-Jones has kindly read the work in typescript and written the Foreword. I value highly his wise counsel and remarkable acumen in the subject of revival.

EIFION EVANS.

CHAPTER 1

PREVIOUS AWAKENINGS

THE eighteenth century Evangelical Revival in Wales was blessed with extraordinary success. The entire life of the nation was deeply influenced by it, and through the length and breadth of the country the pattern of religious life changed fundamentally. A new alignment took place in the denominational affiliation of the majority of professing Christians. Wales had been Protestant for a century or more, but it was due to the revivals of the eighteenth century that it became predominantly nonconformist.

This was substantially consolidated through the smaller, scattered revivals of the first half of the nineteenth century, but notably during the remarkable outpouring of God's Spirit in 1859, when an estimated 110,000 were added to the churches, of which four-fifths were reckoned among the nonconformist ranks.[1] A similar proportion was reported by the royal commission of 1906, which was concerned with obtaining accurate information with a view to giving serious consideration to the question of disestablishing the Welsh Anglican church.[2] It was among this nonconformist community that the main stream of revival blessing flowed in the intervening period between these two estimates. Indeed, it is a noteworthy fact that each of the leaders in three main revivals of the period was connected with the Calvinistic Methodist or Presbyterian Church of Wales—David Morgan, Richard Owen, and Evan Roberts.

Local Revivals in 1866

Local revivals were reported among other denominations. An instance is the season of refreshing experienced at Tredegar in 1866. The English Wesleyan Methodist cause having expired through lack of support from the Welsh-speaking population, responsibility for the small flock and building debt passed to the Independents. Added to these internal problems was the fearfully low moral state of the town, and the Christians set themselves, in covenant together, to pray daily :

> Come, Holy Spirit, heavenly Dove,
> With all thy quickening powers,
> Come, shed abroad a Saviour's love,
> And that shall kindle ours.

The concern intensified and found expression in a week of prayer meetings specifically for revival. Their prayers were answered in a twofold way : "Several revivalists came quite unexpectedly amongst us, and the 'pestilence that walketh in darkness' appeared about the same time". The spread of cholera produced great alarm, and the people flocked to the meetings which were held almost every evening for six months. These continued late into the night, and the sense of conviction of sin was such that people were unable to leave the churches without making their peace with God. The number of young people converted, and their expressions of 'love to Jesus', were especially noteworthy. Some hundred were added to the Independent church alone at that time. The movement was characterized by fervent singing, solid preaching of Christ and His cross, a willingness among the converts for self-denial, and a deep concern that they should grow in grace and in the knowledge of Jesus Christ.[3]

The same year witnessed another awakening in the Aber-avon area of neighbouring Glamorganshire. This was characterized by the fervour of the prayer meetings. These multiplied in number and were attended by increasingly large congregations. The churches became more militant in their witness, the preaching more powerful, and the whole community more conscious of the divine presence and activity. The converts were counted in hundreds and the favourable effects on the life of the churches were lasting.[4]

South Wales 1871

A mere five years later another movement of the Spirit was stirring the churches in certain parts of South Wales, principally the larger centres of population. The churches had felt for some time a crippling deadness of soul, and about 1870, at Newport, a prayer meeting was commenced which met every Friday evening. At first this was poorly attended, and prayers for the success of the means of grace and for a general awakening were offered in the midst of much discouragement. The small band persevered, however, and the prayer meetings grew in numbers and fervency. Shortly afterwards the minister's preaching seemed to become more powerful, and this in turn prompted the members of the prayer meeting to greater expectancy.

Meanwhile similar things were happening in Cardiff, especially under the ministry of Rev. Robert Aitken, Vicar of Pendeen, in Cornwall, who was holding a mission in the city. The movement there was characterized by an intensity of conviction among all classes of people, and "every night crowds of penitents came to God's people for direction. The after-services were prolonged until nearly or quite midnight". During the two weeks of the mission some six hundred made profession of faith, and the desire for a further outpouring of the Holy Spirit increased and spread to several nonconformist churches in the area.

Such was the awareness of eternal issues that in Newport two addresses were delivered daily by Lord Radstock in the Drill Hall to capacity crowds. Robert Aitken continued his mission activity in the same town, and about one thousand converts were counted in a single parish within four months. There were reports of great spiritual concern as far west as Aberavon, which Aitken also visited with much blessing, one token of this preoccupation with eternal issues being the prayer meetings held at 6.30 in the morning. Undoubtedly the leading feature of this work was the number of prayer meetings which sprang up in many Glamorgan towns. The spiritual harvest was reaped in the Rhondda Valleys too, as well as along the southern seaboard.[5]

Visitations in 1887

In 1887 there were revivals further West and North, principally among the Baptists in the county town of Carmarthen, and among the Congregationalists in Blaenau Ffestiniog, Merionethshire. With regard to the former of these places, no awakening could have had a less propitious start. According to custom it was proposed to hold a New Year's week of prayer, but as New Year's Day fell on a Saturday there was considerable scepticism as to the outcome. A mere six persons attended the first meeting, but as the week progressed an awareness of unusual interest gripped the people, and the prayer meetings were eventually continued for nine weeks. There were no visible results at first, but a distinct turning point was felt at one of the meetings, compared to a pentecostal visitation. From that date there was a steady stream of conversions. The total number at that time was 109, including persons of all age groups.[6]

A similar number of conversions was reported from Blaenau Ffestiniog in one week's preaching services. Large congregations attended the prayer meetings which preceded the main preaching service each night, and listened with rapt attention. It was long remembered in the locality for its outstanding success.[7]

Stirrings in the 1890s

At the beginning of the last decade of the century the church at Caersalem, Dowlais, in the upper reaches of Glamorganshire, was in a fearfully low condition. The minister and congregation in the latter half of 1890 covenanted together to pray each day at noon for the unconverted, with startling effects :

"There were clear evidences of the Holy Spirit's working in their midst, with unmistakable signs that the gospel was the power of God unto salvation—the number of those who sought admission into the fellowship of the church being reckoned in tens . . . The awakening lasted for five months . . . and in that festival year 133 were added to the church . . . The neighbouring churches also felt the influences of the awakening."[8]

Prayer also brought blessing to the Baptist church at Pontnewydd in Monmouthshire in the late summer of 1892. The prayer meetings, although quiet and restrained, were nevertheless powerful, and the sense of awe and earnestness intensified during the eight weeks of their continuance. The total number of conversions recorded was 165, of whom 104 were baptized in September before a congregation of some 6,000, and a further 50 the following month. The whole place was solemnized by this work of grace, and religion continued to be the subject of conversation for many months.[9]

It would be misleading to claim for these small-scale, local movements of the Holy Spirit any significant and lasting influence in the background to the revival of 1904. Nevertheless at a time of almost general declension they did keep alive in the minds, as well as the hearts, of the people of God the divine pattern for carrying forward the work of His kingdom.

Richard Owen, the revivalist

It was the Richard Owen revival, however, which caused the widest stir, and left the most lasting impact on the nation as a whole in the period between the two great movements of God in 1859 and 1904. Even though his revival activity was mainly confined chronologically to the early '80s, and geographically to North Wales, his own claim was 13,000 souls won for Christ under the blessing of God, and when he died in 1887, at the early age of forty-eight, 'Richard Owen the revivalist', was a household name throughout the Principality.[10]

The chief means of enlightening Richard Owen in the way of salvation was the early influence of a godly home. His father, a farmer in Anglesey, died when Richard was only eleven years of age, and this, together with the death of his elder brother a year later, contributed to the meagreness of the education he received. Family worship, memorizing scripture, and especially the loving, Christ-like tenderness of his father's piety made eternal issues real to him early in life, so that he was received as a communicant member in the local Calvinistic Methodist Church before he entered his teens. Reminiscing on this period he says :

"I had committed a great deal of the Bible to memory while yet very young, and the verses began speaking to me. I would have most pleasure when in church. Under a good sermon

I could hardly contain myself without weeping much when, as would often happen, it was delivered with power; and sometimes I was unable to resist the desire to praise God for the plan to save guilty sinners."[11]

From step to step he made progress in grace and knowledge, the church recognizing his God-given gifts in making him a Sunday School teacher, and in the positions of responsibility and leadership associated with that work. These different avenues of Christian work brought upon him an increasing conviction of God's call to preach the gospel, a conviction which received added impetus at the time of the 1859 revival. He was twenty at the time and the sense of God's call had been with him for some four years.

On his visit to Llangristiolus (Anglesey), where Richard Owen worshipped, David Morgan (the revivalist of 1859) witnessed some of the most remarkable scenes of that extraordinary visitation. At the close of Morgan's meeting there was a keen sense of disappointment in the lack of response to the message, at which the revivalist expressed no surprise, claiming that the church was spiritually disqualified to foster any converts. This is how the meeting continued :

"Some of you have intimated your desire for the Holy Spirit. I would like to know whether there are any who have longed for Him sufficiently to lose a night's sleep in order to pray for Him." Then he asked several in the church individually and received a negative reply until he came to one old man near the door who replied "No, I have never done so, but I have decided that I will." "Here is one who promises to do so," said the revivalist, "is there any one who will join him?" "Yes," exclaimed the young Richard Owen . . . The revivalist then went on his knees praying for the converts, and those who had made the above promise, and for the church. . . . While praying for the church, suddenly "there came a sound from heaven as of a rushing mighty wind, and it filled all the house where they were sitting."

At this point in the meeting nearly everyone was overcome by the powerful influences, and they were shouting their praises without restraint or sequence. This did not last long, and it was exactly a week later that while Richard Owen was praying with some of the young people there was an ecstatic outburst of joyful praise. The news spread quickly and the families of the surrounding scattered farms gathered to join in the meeting, which went on until 2 o'clock the following morning. The spiritual harvest numbered some ninety added to the churches of the Calvinistic Methodists and Independents.[12]

Once the decisive step of submitting himself as candidate for the ministry had been taken, Richard Owen had to apply himself to study, preaching and farming at the same time. Subsequently he spent some time at the denominational theological college at Bala, married, and moved to London. Here he spent two years preaching to the congregation of Calvinistic Methodists which met at Tollington Hall, inspiring them to build their own church at Holloway, and towards the end of that time, in 1873, he was ordained to the full work of the ministry. Returning to his native Anglesey he gave himself "to prayer and the ministry of the Word."

In the years that followed he became increasingly aware of the need for a ministry wider than his prescribed circuit of preaching stations. Probably through the kindness of Mrs. Anne Davies (wife of an Anglesey M.P. and daughter of Henry Rees, one of the leaders of the Calvinistic Methodists until his death in 1869), Richard Owen, together with many other nonconformist ministers, was enabled to go to

Liverpool in the February of 1875 to hear D. L. Moody. The Welsh preacher already had Moody's message : now he was interested in Moody's methods. Moody taught him plainness and directness, and increased his sense of responsibility and zeal towards the unconverted. Nevertheless it was David Morgan's pattern that Richard Owen followed, as being more suitable to the traditional Welsh manner of conducting divine service. This meant that after the sermon, prayer was offered and an exhortation given, and then an announcement that a church meeting would follow where an invitation would be given for those who wished to make a profession of faith. He came to regard a closing hymn as an intrusion upon the impression left by the message and unconducive to its bearing fruit in due course. Together with two other ministers he began to spend more time in prayer, and early in 1876 they commenced their mission in a dwindling congregation at Llain-goch, Holyhead.

The prayer meeting on the second afternoon was unexpectedly full. Towards the end of the meeting Richard Owen announced a hymn, but such an awareness of the divine presence overpowered him that he could only give the first couplet. He tried many times to go through the first verse, and each failure intensified the sense of awe in the congregation. When he eventually succeeded in reciting the complete verse, which was about the certainty of the fulfilment in the divine purpose of the shedding of Christ's blood, the whole congregation was melted to tears and silent weeping. This shattering silence prevailed until a godly dockworker who had come in his working clothes cried out in heartfelt thanksgiving. Throughout the week of preaching services that followed the whole town was filled with concern over spiritual and eternal issues, the meetings were overcrowded, and sixty in all professed faith in Jesus Christ.

The meetings were continued for a further period in a larger church with similar results.

Associated with Richard Owen in his early evangelistic efforts was John Richard Hughes, at that time pastor of the Calvinistic Methodist cause, Armenia, in Holyhead. His sustained vision and burning zeal as an evangelist found militant expression in untiring service. Whether in the isolated hamlets of Anglesey or in the expanding townships straddled on either side of Offa's Dyke, he had equal facility in communicating the message of saving grace. For much of the latter half of the nineteenth century he was the spearhead of his denomination's home mission work in the border area, labouring with little official recognition but with much and lasting success.[13]

From Holyhead the team of evangelists went further afield in Anglesey, and their ministry was blessed to the conversion of between 250 and 300 at that time. Turning to South Wales they laboured in many of the mining valleys with the same unction attending their preaching, so that by the end of the year about 800 had been brought to a saving knowledge of Christ.

It was in the years 1882 and 1883, however, that the revival which bears his name really broke out, especially in Caernarvonshire. The Calvinistic Methodists alone could speak of an increase in 1882 of 680, and in 1883 of 784 persons. Village after village was visited by the revivalist, usually for a week of preaching services, often preceded by prayer meetings and followed by powerful influences among young and old. Whole communities were plunged into severe conviction of sin and fear of wrath and judgment. Strong men spent nights restless with remorse because of past blasphemy and unbelief, until they were brought to gospel liberty, when their joy knew no bounds and their praises drowned the preacher's voice. The very tone of the worship was changed in many churches, even as men's lives were changed by the power of God. This was especially true of the fellowship meeting, the "seiat", where it was customary to relate and examine the spiritual experiences of the saints. After the revival not only was the "seiat" numerically stronger; it was truly experimental with clear evidences of life, righteousness, peace and joy in the Holy Ghost.

In the midst of it Richard Owen spoke of a whole countryside aflame for God. It was *the* subject of conversation; in the home, on the road, at work, the absorbing topic was always "the holy fire" which had descended from heaven itself. Somehow the whole country seemed to have heard of this divine visitation overnight, for without design or publicity hundreds flocked to the various villages week after week from great distances.

Almost at the centre of the Lleyn peninsula lies the little village of Nant, and at the closing service of Richard Owen's visit, the first Sunday of 1883, he was preaching on Isaiah 55:1, "Ho, every one that thirsteth, come ye to the waters, and he that hath no money; come ye, buy, and eat." There was as large a congregation outside the building as inside it, and with the windows opened all were able to join in the worship. The effects of the preaching were among the most powerful witnessed by the people during the entire revival :

"The faces of many were bathed in tears; the faces of others shone with joy, and the 'Amen' of people repeatedly drowned the preacher's voice. He invited the hearers to the feast with the most pressing urgency, saying, 'The picnic lunches of salvation are ready—come and take them, friends. You will be eternally rich if you come, and forever miserable if you do not come; dear people, come! Tonight is a con-

venient season; your packs are all ready and prepared on the
counter of mercy, and Christ expects you. Dear people, come
to-night! . . .' The whole place resounded to the cry of
Amen from every quarter. A church meeting was called for
at the close of the service, and when silence was obtained,
many had remained, seventeen of them for the first time."[14]

Passing from Caernarvonshire to the neighbouring
Merionethshire in April, 1883, there was no abatement in the
power or extent of the influences. Indeed, they continued
throughout the remainder of that year, and into the following
year when Owen laboured in Denbighshire and Flintshire,
returning eventually through Merionethshire to his native
Anglesey, where he laboured with eminent success in 1884
and 1885. As a result of one meeting in Denbigh, over a
hundred were converted out of an estimated congregation of
about 3,000, and the number of persons converted in the town
during that period was 430 in all.

Richard Owen claimed no recipe for success. His educational attainments were non-existent, and although he followed
closely the same pattern of meeting in each place he visited,
prayer before the services, and the closing address rather than
the closing hymn, yet it was in no sense carried out mechanic-
ally, or as a matter of technique, but from conviction and in
simple dependence on the Holy Spirit for success. His
preaching was orthodox in its matter, dwelling especially on
the divine provision of salvation through the crucified Son of
God and on individual responsibility, together with a pressing
urgency in the application of the message. Simple and forth-
right in manner, his appeal was to the common folk, and under
the blessing of God he was signally used to awaken and renew
a wide area of the Lord's vineyard in North Wales. Although
restricted in these ways, the Richard Owen revival not only

infused new life into countless churches, and reaped a substantial harvest of souls for the kingdom of God, but also kept alive in the sanctified memories of God's people the need for "a season of refreshing from the presence of the Lord."

It is true that both the Richard Owen and the 1904 revivals were preceded by the work of American evangelists, and the former work was closely associated with the man whose name it bears, the blessings being confined almost exclusively in the '80s to his ministry. Nevertheless, these Welsh movements of the Spirit were initiated by divine, rather than human, means. During the period of their duration there were manifest tokens of general awakening and renewal in the life of the church, as well as the conversion of ungodly men. A spontaneity and irresistible power were much in evidence, and sustained impressions of the divine presence and activity were made upon whole neighbourhoods. Furthermore, the intensity and reality of the spiritual experiences of those days distinguished them from the realm of ordinary campaigning evangelism, however extensive, and marked them out as extraordinary visitations of the Spirit of God. It is important to draw the distinction, for all too often the Welsh movements were wrongly interpreted in terms of Moody.

CHAPTER 2

EVANGELISTIC AGENCIES

MENTION has already been made of the impression
made on some of the North Wales preachers during
Moody's visit to Liverpool in 1875. He also visited Cardiff
and Swansea some seven years later, and the particular
flavour of the Moody and Sankey methods was further publi-
cized throughout Wales by the efforts of John Roberts, who
obtained permission from Sankey to translate his hymns into
Welsh and prepare suitable musical arrangements for them.
Another twenty years passed before the Torrey Alexander
team duplicated the methods and enjoyed much the same
success in various centres, including Cardiff.

John Pugh and the Forward Movement

Although related to some of Moody's methods, there
sprang up in South Wales from 1872 onwards an indigenous
work of church extension character, which, in thirty years,
grew to the unpredictable proportions of forty-eight centres
of worship with a total seating capacity of over forty-two
thousand. The architect of this "Forward Movement" of the
Presbyterian Church of Wales, as it came to be called, was
John Pugh, who in 1872 became minister of a languishing
church at Tredegar. Within a month of his being inducted
to the charge Pugh realized that if he was going to "fulfil his
ministry" and "do the work of an evangelist" he would have
to venture forth to meet the unconverted on their own ground.

In practical terms, this meant an open-air meeting at the
town clock, a delicate and somewhat dangerous strategy, even

though the position was central. It was delicate because many of the traditional religionists raised their eyebrows at what was to them a casting of pearls before swine. It was dangerous because of an uncomfortable precedent to which Pugh referred in his opening statements :

"Boys, they tell me that you are an awful set here, and that you were in the habit of throwing rotten eggs at the head, and mud into the mouth, of a dear old minister who used to stand up here and tell you of Jesus and His love. I am not afraid of anyone in this crowd, but I am awfully afraid of myself, for if any of you should insult me and I lose my temper, I should surely mark that man."[1]

He was assured vocally of at least one supporter and the meeting continued in peace. As a result of this venture much success attended Pugh's ministry, and the congregation grew to such an extent that it was necessary to hire the Temperance Hall with its seating accommodation for one thousand, and this was regularly filled on Sunday evenings.

From Tredegar, Pugh went to Pontypridd, another mining town with much the same religious indifference. Here he carried on the open-air ministry and met some opposition. The town crier was hired to ring his bell, and later a brass band to perform, at the time of the meeting. Fired with the vision of countless numbers rescued from immorality, indifference, crime, and profligacy by means of such militant evangelism, Pugh removed to Cardiff in 1889. Meanwhile his friendship with Rev. William Ross of Cowcaddens Free Church, Glasgow, had crystallized in his mind the means to be used under God to make the vision a reality.

Ross had met with extraordinary success in that destitute area. He had been under no illusion as to the urgent need for tireless evangelistic activity on the part of the church, and his programme ran along the following lines :

1. The church to be opened every night of the week.
2. Every member of the church to do active Christian work at home and in public.
3. Open-air mission to be organised on a large scale.
4. Work to be organised among the young people and children.
5. Workers to have an opportunity of consulting frequently and of being thoroughly trained from time to time in their work.
6. Above all that the church should seek the Spirit of God and consecration, and regard it as the highest honour and privilege to be employed in the interest of the kingdom.[2]

The Welsh work under Pugh followed the principles, if not the details, of this scheme. The difference lay in the wider scope of Pugh's "Forward Movement", for he envisaged taking the spiritual conflict into the enemy's camp not only in Cardiff but throughout Wales. Gradually the pattern emerged in his mind; it would be necessary to carry out the work in stages. First the initial campaigning, militant evangelism; and secondly the establishment of more permanent areas of worship suitable to the needs of the converts. This would necessitate zealous workers, financial backing, and the denomination's support. He found all three.

Seth and Frank Joshua

In Seth Joshua he found a fellow-worker of the most indefatigable kind. Joshua was a colourful character, the spiritual counterpart of his illustrious biblical namesake.

When Pugh challenged him with the evangelistic proposal that was weighing on his mind, Joshua had been converted for ten years and, together with his brother Frank, was an experienced campaigner in the field of home missions.

Both Seth and Frank Joshua were converted at a Salvation Army meeting. This may account for the virility of their evangelism, into which they were plunged almost immediately. At Neath they gave themselves wholly to the task of saving souls; they sang and prayed, they sold Bibles at the pleasure fair, held open-air meetings near public houses, faced opposition and ridicule, and in the midst of it all found time to read theology from such Puritan writers as Richard Sibbes and Thomas Manton. Consequently, their evangelism, though popular in its appeal, was far from superficial in its content or temporary in its results.

An example of Seth's conversational style in preaching is given by W. Nantlais Williams in his reminiscences :

"While urging men to Christ at the close of one meeting, he sought to forestall the objections of some. 'I would come to Christ to-night,' you say, 'if I knew I was one of the elect.' 'Friend,' said Seth, 'where do you find that word "election"?' 'O! Mr. Joshua in the Epistle to the Romans.' 'My dear friend,' Seth continued, 'that letter was not written to you, but to Christians. You read the Gospels, friend. Open your own letters, please'."[3]

His faith was entirely in God and in His message rather than in men and their methods. When faced with the question, twenty years after the revival, "Is there hope for the gospel obtaining again a hold of the masses in South Wales?", his reply was unequivocal. "The people are crying out for it. There is no grip in anything else . . . The people are sick and tired of the present-day attempts to dress up the gospel in new clothes. A new tribe of theological tailors have wearied the people by forcing the gospel to become a quick-change artist."[4]

It was in response to Pugh's appeal that he came to Cardiff, bringing with him a wife and family of six (with no financial guarantee for their maintenance) and the important item of one large, spacious tent. This was to be pitched at the very walls of an impregnable Jericho, the Splott district of Cardiff. There was no shortage of critics : "You might as well try to demolish the Fort of Gibraltar with boiled peas as to convert the people of Splott in a tent." Undaunted by such quips Joshua set to work erecting the tent, and just as he was finishing it the following conversation with a passer-by took place :

" 'Hello, Guvnor, what is this, a boxing show?' 'There is going to be some fighting here.' 'When are you going to start?' 'To-morrow morning at 11 o'clock.' 'To-morrow's Sunday,' he said. 'Well, better the day, better the deed.' 'Who's on?' 'I have got to take on the first round.' 'Who's with you?' 'Well, he's a chap called Beelzebub.' 'Never heard of him; who is he?' 'Oh, he is a smart one, I can tell you; come tomorrow morning.' 'I will be there, guvnor' . . ."

Joshua completes the tale : "Strange to say he was there. When I had given out the first hymn, 'All hail the power of Jesu's name,' he knew he was caught. Old Beelzebub went over the ropes all right, for that chap was converted that very morning."[5]

Incidents such as these were typical in the early years of the Forward Movement. They stemmed from the unquenchable zeal of Pugh and Joshua to take the gospel to people wherever they were to be found in their spiritual need and danger.

From Cardiff the work spread to other industrial centres

of populations, the Rhondda Valley, Merthyr, Newport, Swansea, extending as far as Wrexham in North Wales before the turn of the century. This rapid development was possible through the financial assistance of John Cory, a wealthy Cardiff coal merchant, and Edward Davies of Llandinam, eminent landowner and philanthropist. At the General Assembly of the Presbyterian Church of Wales Pugh's work was officially recognized and sanctioned as meeting an urgent need in the more densely populated areas of Wales. He was freed from pastoral oversight and appointed missioner, and the work was to be brought to the notice of all the churches to solicit their prayerful support, as well as to put the work on a secure and healthy financial basis.

The denomination was compelled to recognize the unmistakable affinities between Pugh's efforts and those of the early Calvinistic Methodist fathers. In their generation they had felt the same overwhelming constraint to take the gospel to people in their sin at all cost. By 1906 the Forward Movement churches could number nearly seven thousand communicant members, over one thousand on probation and some twenty-two thousand hearers. Apart from the fact that Seth Joshua's ministry was blessed to Evan Roberts at a crucial time in his dealings with God, as will be shown later, the distinctive character of the Forward Movement work made it a vehicle eminently suited to advance the 1904 revival.

The coming of the Salvation Army to the mining valleys of Glamorganshire in 1879 made a tremendous impact on the people. Its militant evangelistic and social programme stirred the churches from their lethargic indifference, and they became more vigorous not only in their praying but also in their missionary effort. Numerous conversions were reported from the ranks of the careless and ungodly, there was a marked decrease in drunkenness, and the campaigning mood of the churches was freely discussed in homes and shops, at work and on the streets.[6]

Rosina Davies

One woman in particular who was influenced by the Salvation Army was Rosina Davies.[7] From that time forward she gave herself unsparingly to holding missions throughout the Principality. Vyrnwy Morgan spoke of her contribution in twenty years of such work in this way :

"Wherever she went, it was in the spirit of a servant, freely giving the best that was in her to every sect, imposing no conditions save the intercessory prayers of the faithful, with no thought of self, and no expectation of gain, co-operating with ministers, melting the multitudes by her sincerity and the magic of her songs, touching the most selfish and indifferent by the pathos and tenderness of her prayers, and proclaiming the love of God and the grandeur of the Nazarene."[8]

In her missions she often witnessed between twenty and fifty conversions in a meeting; during one Sunday's services as many as eighty-four, and on at least one occasion a whole family was converted at the same meeting.[9]

Rosina Davies travelled extensively for this purpose. Early in 1904 she exercised a very fruitful ministry in Rhos, near Wrexham,[10] later to prove one of the most richly blessed centres of the revival. Many journeyed from distant Glamorganshire to her meetings at the Congregational church of New Quay in August, and at one of the meetings, according to Elvet Lewis, "the manifestation of power was exceptional."[11] During her meetings at Gelli in the Rhondda Valley the following month nineteen conversions were recorded; the church was too small to hold the crowds, and many of the congregation were overcome by uncontrollable weeping.[12]

When the revival had become generally widespread, her mission work continued as far afield as Holywell and Colwyn Bay on the North Wales coast. Here again the churches were too small to contain the vast crowds which flocked to the meetings, many of the services being prolonged to the early hours of the morning.[13] This remarkable woman showed unflagging energy and devotion in the work of the revival, and even in March 1905 was holding a week's meetings at Caernarvon, with no little success.[14]

Jessie Penn-Lewis

Jessie Penn-Lewis was another woman who became prominent during the revival. Her father, Samuel Jones, was a Calvinistic Methodist minister at Neath, Glamorganshire. She married when only nineteen and soon afterwards "began to feel very ill at ease about the Lord's return." This resulted in her conversion on New Year's Day, 1882. On their removal to Richmond, Surrey, the young couple found great spiritual profit under the ministry of Evan H. Hopkins. Two years later she solemnly consecrated herself fully to Christ's service.

She continued to hunger for more of God, and felt her failure keenly in one particular outlet of service. This was her extreme nervousness in leading a Bible class. She felt that the answer lay in a deeper experience of the Holy Spirit, and she came to a fuller understanding of Romans 6 :6-11. She later described the result of this deeper realization of God's provision for the believer in the cross :

"(1) It was sudden, and when I was not specially thinking about the matter. (2) I knew in my spirit that He had come. (3) My Bible became like a living thing and was flooded with light. (4) Christ suddenly became to me a real Person : I could not explain how I knew, but He became real to me. (5) When I went to my Bible Class, I found myself able to speak with liberty of utterance, with the conviction of the Spirit at the back of it, until souls were convicted of sin on every side. (6) Power in prayer, so that it seemed I only needed to ask and have. (7) My spirit took its way to God, freed from every fetter that held to anything on earth."[15]

About this time she read the *Life of Madame Guyon* and this, together with a visit to the Keswick Convention in 1892, exerted a profound influence on her life.

Liberated from nervous tensions in public ministry, her success in Y.W.C.A. work at Richmond, Neath, and other places encouraged her to attend a Y.W.C.A. conference in Sweden. This was the first of many overseas journeys before the end of the century. She also busied herself with several books on the theme of the believer's identification with Christ :

"That the cross 'breaks the power of cancelled sin' through the identification of the sinner with Christ in His death to sin and to the world; that 'crucified with Christ', the believer is led into a fellowship with Christ that alone enables him to obey the Lord's injunction to 'take up the cross and follow Me', with all that this involves in conformity to the likeness of the Lamb."[16]

Indeed, this aspect of the cross became her consuming passion. In addition to her literary work she spoke at several Keswick Conventions.

Her insistence on "the message of the cross" grew to such proportions—J. C. Pollock refers to her ministry as "rather-one-tracked"[17]—that she withdrew her active participation in and support of Keswick itself in 1909, and of the Welsh Keswick at Llandrindod two years later. Her biographer gives as the reason that the "truth to be unfolded needed the full time of a convention for its elucidation, and it could no longer be faithfully made known in occasional addresses and side meetings".[18]

In the midst of all this activity there were those made lonely by the anguish of dissatisfaction at their spiritual progress and ministerial uselessness. There were six ministers in particular who felt the need for a convention in Wales along Keswick lines, and for six years from 1896 several Christians had prayed specifically for it. Eventually the Welsh Keswick was engineered by Mrs. Jessie Penn-Lewis to take place at Llandrindod Wells in the summer of 1903. Among those who were blessed at that time were R. B. Jones (who preached with great effect at Rhos in 1904) and W. W. Lewis (who was widely used in a teaching ministry before and during the revival). These and others proceeded to hold conventions in various parts of the country for the express purpose of "deepening of the spiritual life." Emphasis was placed on entire consecration to God and implicit submission to the Holy Spirit. Many entered into a new realization of communion with God by these means, one such being E. Keri Evans of Carmarthen, whose reminiscences, *Fy Mhererindod Ysbrydol* (My Spiritual Pilgrimage), published in 1938, became a religious classic, and whose teaching ministry was signally useful to succeeding generations of young converts.[19]

R. B. Jones

R. B. Jones was a Baptist minister. After his ordination in 1893 he had served pastorates at Berthlwyd and Llanelli before his removal to Porth in the Rhondda valley, where he was ministering in 1904. Together with others he had felt a definite lack in his ministry, and in a postscript to one of his letters he gave expression to his longing at that time: "Oh, how great the need to be filled with the Holy Spirit. I believe that it is a tide in the order of God. If we are caught in the flood, we shall be blessed with great success in our work."[20] They decided to seek help from F. B. Meyer, but as he expected to minister at Llandrindod in the first Welsh Keswick Convention that year it was agreed to attend the meetings there.

Three weeks after his visit to Llandrindod, Jones came into great personal blessing. Writing to O. M. Owen he shared the experience :

"I am, thank God, out in the light with you. At last I am able to exercise that simple faith and trust in God's promises and truth. This power has been given me to overcome numerous temptations. Oh, how sweet it is to pray ! What a wonderful book the Bible has become ! Formerly, it was a collection of texts, now its every word is fraught with a message to me personally. Wherever one turns on receiving this experience, one is filled with the wonder of it all, and is not the greatest wonder received when one thinks that he was contented to be so long without it, and how wonderfully simple it is—Jesus living in me? In consequence of my self-surrender to Him, I am His and He is mine ... I have simply to repeat and plead His promise and trust Him to get me through safely and Lo, it is done ! . . . I am waiting for more and there is more, more, and more. Oh, for a life of thorough dependence upon the Lord and great faithfulness to His will !"[21]

Members of this group subsequently travelled widely in Wales holding "revival missions", their messages and appeal being in the words of R. B. Jones, "almost exclusively to those within the church. The call was to holiness." Speaking of the results he says : "Cwmbach, Dowlais, Llwynypia, Peny-darren, Porth, Cefnmawr, Cwmavon and Pencoed are only some of the places where the fires of revival burned glowingly, but as yet, not in such form as to attract the attention of the press. The spectacular was an element entirely absent from this mighty work of the Spirit."[22] The activities of these ministers were mainly directed as expressed, towards the faithful remnant in the churches of that period.

The "United Evangelical Mission"

Apart from the work of individual evangelists, the British Free Church Council called upon its constituent bodies to arrange a "United Evangelical Mission" in the spring of 1901. This was to be a concerted effort throughout the land, beginning with London in January and extending to the country areas by March. While it is difficult to estimate the practical value of the mission, notice was taken by the Calvinistic Methodists of the arrangements, and the churches were urged, in the words of the North Wales Association's minutes, "to join heartily with all other Christians in holding evangelistic and temperance meetings during the appointed period".

Inevitably, such a resolution met with only limited success. Its implementation was awkward in a situation where the churches looked upon the Home Mission (working among the Welsh near-exiles of the English border towns) and Forward Movement (working in the industrial centres of South Wales) as their evangelistic agencies. Evangelism, in the technical sense of outreach, had thus been conveniently departmentalized and depersonalized. It was no longer looked upon as the function of the local congregation, but rather as the responsibility of a denominational committee. The vision of perishing souls seemed relevant only to the far-away citadels of paganism. The church at large failed to see that judgment would have to begin at a house of God nearer at hand.

The problem, however, concerned not merely the agency of evangelism but also its meaning and implications. Attention was being diverted from the traditionally dogmatic categories of sin, atonement, regeneration and sanctification to the more pragmatic considerations of human progress, universal brotherhood, social consciousness and what were deemed the over-riding considerations of a "practical Christianity". With this new emphasis, evangelism in a local situation soon lost its virility and urgency, and by implication men were no longer convinced of its necessity.

Previous Welsh revivals had taken place in the context of an accepted, even if at times sterile, orthodoxy. By 1904 those very doctrines which had formed the backbone of the historic denominations were relegated to a place of secondary importance. If they were not strenuously opposed, at least they were regarded with scornful indifference. Having, in the eyes of religious leaders, lost their significance and relevance to a progressive society, these vital truths were culpably ignored in the preaching and teaching ministry of the churches. Consequently the 1904 revival came to a church which was doctrinally off balance. Sadly, there were to be few who had either the discernment or the conviction to correct it.

CHAPTER 3

THEOLOGICAL DECLINE

REVIVAL is variously described in the Bible. Occasionally it is under the figure of a divine conflagration, bringing mercy as well as judgment; again, as floods on dry ground, not to drown, but to assuage; it may be as a whirlwind bearing all before it, to build rather than demolish; or as a healthy vigorous growth of supernatural rather than natural origin. Sometimes the movement is traced from a well-defined source; more often it is the effects which receive attention from the inspired authors. In between cause and effect the details are sketched sparsely, often roughly, always with wonder. For revival is a work of grace; the prime mover, the initiator and supervisor of this divine activity is consistently and invariably shown to be God the Holy Spirit.

Repeatedly these seasons of refreshing from the presence of the Lord emerge in the providence of God at a time of crisis. When true religion is at a premium, when the Word of God is scarce and the lamp of God burns low in the land, then it is that the irresistible energies of the eternal Spirit burst forth with a vigour seldom witnessed more than once in any one generation. In the midst of the spiritual deadness there has always been a faithful remnant who had wisdom to discern and compassion to mourn the languishing state. It is possible in historical perspective to trace the earliest stirrings of new life even before the evidences of revival became general. So it is with the "Welsh Revival of 1904", variously described as the "Evan Roberts Revival" (after one of its leading

35

figures), "the 1904 Revival" (after the date of its climax), or simply "the Revival" (being the last widespread movement of its kind in Wales).

It is true that the extensive publicity accompanying the revival through the medium of the press attracted the attention of observers and visitors from the rest of the British Isles, most European countries including Scandinavia, and even America. In spite of the language difficulty, Welsh being the chief medium of expression, many flocked to witness the phenomena, if not to obtain the fire for themselves and, through them, for others. While therefore many were interested in this radical outburst of revivalism, from different standpoints and for different reasons, it took place against the backcloth of spiritual decline in the life of the churches. It is important to realize that this declension affected theological, denominational, and moral issues.

For many years the 1904 Revival was looked upon as nothing more than a "much ado about nothing" because of its emotionalism. The advocates of this view have been many, from the Rev. Peter Price who caused a furore at the time by referring to the revival as the product of fleshly rather than heavenly fire, to the writer who brought forth a vigorous protest from W. Ambrose Bebb some fifty years later. Bebb's rebuttal of the charge that the ineffectiveness of the Welsh churches in the 1950s was due to that "wind of emotionalism, the 1904-05 revival", is made to rest largely on the theological delinquency of the ministers and preachers during the decade prior to the revival.[1] During that period the full impact of the liberalizing tendencies in theology from within the ranks of professing Christendom was felt in Wales chiefly, if not solely, in the theological colleges and among the ministers trained by them. To trace its source, however, it is necessary to go back a little further.

The rise of liberalism

It was Bishop Robinson in his sensational *Honest to God* who found an analogy between his unorthodox "defence of the faith" and that of a similar attempt almost exactly a century before his controversial publication appeared. The "guardians of traditional orthodoxy" at that time were in Robinson's view "too conservative", and "all but rendered impossible the true defence of the gospel."[2] The champions of orthodoxy in 1862 had been at pains to refute the advanced liberal views of J. W. Colenso, then bishop of Natal, South Africa, in his book *The Pentateuch and the Book of Joshua Critically Examined* which appeared in that year. H. D. McDonald notes that the volume "caused bitter antagonism. For the first time a bishop's name was associated with what was regarded as open infidelity."[3] The advocacy of biblical criticism of the most destructive, negative kind gathered momentum throughout the latter half of the nineteenth century. It received no little impetus from the publication of Charles Darwin's *Origin of Species* which appeared in 1859, by transposing its evolutionary theories from the scientific realm to that of revelation. By this means faith in the Bible as the Word of God was gradually undermined. The years which followed Darwin's monumental book also saw the rise of the new goddess of science, and optimism as to the possibilities that lay ahead for man rose to a high level.

Essays and Reviews, which appeared in 1860, was in many ways the fore-runner of a whole class of literature having a radical, liberalizing purpose. One of the contributors, Rowland Williams, the Professor of Hebrew at Lampeter College, a position of influence in the Church of Wales, strongly advocated acceptance of the most advanced German higher criticism.[4]   Later came W. Robertson Smith, "who really popularized Old Testament German criticism" with his article on the "Bible" in the ninth edition of the *Encyclopaedia Britannica,* and through a book on *The Old Testament in the Jewish Church* which appeared in 1881. The Free Church of Scotland courageously disciplined Smith, and he was deprived of his professorial chair of Old Testament at Aberdeen.[5] The fusion of evolutionary hypotheses with higher criticism of the Bible bore fruit in the appearance of another notoriously radical book, edited by Charles Gore, called *Lux Mundi* (1889). Its emphases were upon evolution rather than revelation, the incarnation rather than the atonement, Christ's humanity rather than His deity, and the basic presuppositions of its contributors were fundamentally alien to traditional, supernatural Christianity.[6]

It was the acceptance of ideas such as these among Baptist leaders that initiated the Down-grade Controversy in which Spurgeon was so intimately involved, and which led to his eventual resignation from the Baptist Union in 1888. In the September 1887 issue of his magazine, *The Sword And The Trowel,* he has crystallized the issue :

"Inspiration and speculation cannot long abide in peace. Compromise there can be none. We cannot hold the inspiration of the Word, and yet reject it; we cannot believe in the atonement and deny it; we cannot hold the doctrine of the fall and yet talk of the evolution of spiritual life from human nature; we cannot recognize the punishment of the impenitent and yet indulge the 'larger hope'. One way or the other we must go. Decision is the virtue of the hour."[7]

It was at this point that the churches failed and their declension became inevitable. The subjectivism of Schleiermacher's theology was reaping its twin fruit : speculative criti-

cism of the Bible and psychological interpretation of Christian
experience.

The advent of psychology

During the latter period of the nineteenth century the new
science of psychology attracted an ever increasing and devoted
following, one of its chief exponents being William James.
Books on the subject by this author had appeared regularly
during the '90s. His classical interpretation on psychological
principles of religious experiences appeared as printed lectures
in 1902 under the title *The Varieties of Religious Experience*.
To William James religion was primarily a biological reaction,
and conversion in its essence was generally nothing more than
"a normal adolescent phenomenon."[8] In this essentially
Christian experience of regeneration James failed to recognize
a divine activity related to the gravity of human sin and the
objectivity of divine revelation. In his mind the religious
experience belonged to the realm of subconscious emotional
excitement, and it became theologically fashionable to regard
this interpretation as authentic and adequate.

Consequently many of those converted in the revival which
followed two years later were confronted with philosophic
rather than biblical categories for the understanding of their
experiences. This could not fail to be detrimental to the
quality of their subsequent Christian lives, and so to the
eventual outcome and "image" of the revival as a whole. It
is not in vain that the Scripture speaks of avoiding the "op-
positions of science falsely so called" (1 Timothy 6:20).

By the turn of the century this theological culture had made
substantial inroads into the Welsh orthodox camp. While its
progress had been slow and its impact on the Welsh ministry
delayed, there are clear indications that by 1904 wide areas of
theological influence had been captured for liberalism. Welsh

orthodoxy was fighting a rearguard action, and its exponents were very much on the defensive.

The influence of evolutionary theory

Some writers made the wildest claims in advocating acceptance of the evolutionary principle in the theological disciplines. One of these, writing in 1899, called on theology to "acknowledge its indebtedness in a special way to science", and stated categorically that "the Church's teaching about God, man, and God's relationship to man and to the creation cannot be understood without realizing the marked influence of recent science on theology". Referring to E. Griffith Jones's *Ascent Through Christ,* he claimed that "the discovery (of evolution) revealed man's dignity and glory in a new light . . . that the perfecting of man is the highest goal of all God's works in nature."[9] The inference was clear: the Bible's teaching was irrelevant (because man could only be fully understood in the light of evolution), and Christ's work was insufficient (since the evolutionary process was necessary to bring man to perfection).

Chief among these writers was David Adams. In 1884 he won first prize at the National Eisteddfod for an essay on Hegel, and in 1893 for another essay (in Welsh) on "The Fall, the Incarnation, and the Resurrection in the light of Evolution." The whole thrust of this essay was the application of evolutionary principles to spiritual values, resulting in making the Fall an achievement rather than a catastrophe, and reducing the incarnation from the realm of supernatural intervention to natural development. An inevitable corollary of this position appeared in his book *Moeseg Cristionogol* (Christian Ethics) which maintained that the significance of Christ lay in His teaching about the fatherhood of God rather than in the uniqueness of His person and sacrifice. Another book of his, *Paul yng ngoleuni'r Iesu* (Paul in the Light of Jesus), which appeared in 1897, probably had a wider public. It was an attempt to discredit and belittle Paul's epistles as being incompatible with the simple teaching of Jesus as recorded in the Gospels.[10] The direct, if not desired, effect of these new ideas was the creation of a theological near-vacuum which had neither an objective standard of truth nor a substantial framework of doctrinal reference.

Higher criticism

Higher criticism of the Bible was also having its blighting effect by 1904. Even an able theologian like Dr. Lewis Edwards, Principal of Bala Theological College for the crucial period from 1837 to his death fifty years later, while defending the traditional view of the Bible, compromised with his opponents by doing so from the same philosophic, rational presuppositions. Thus, although his conclusions were different from those of the higher critics, the effect on the wider Christian public was subtle and demoralising. It could hardly be otherwise, for he was using the weapons of the flesh to defend the citadel of the Spirit. If the Bible was vulnerable in a way that necessitated a scintillating scholarship to defend it, the believer's experience of the inward confirmatory testimony of the Holy Spirit to the Bible's divine origin, together with the relevant affirmation of the doctrinal standards traditionally accepted by the churches, was of doubtful value indeed.

Lewis Edwards' strength and weakness lay in his scholasticism, and his affinities lay more with the intricate philosophizing of the mediaeval ages than with the solid biblicism of the puritan fathers. "Let it be remembered that Lewis Edwards was a scholar," says one commentator, "and so he could not rest on a pietistic faith after the pattern of many of

his contemporaries in Wales."[11] Paradoxically, therefore, the
faith of many in the integrity of the Bible was being undermined not only in spite of, but even because of the reasoned
defence of its most learned advocate.

Perhaps the most effective attempt at stemming the liberal
tide was an address delivered by J. Cynddylan Jones from
the Moderator's chair of the General Assembly of the Presbyterian Church of Wales in 1902. It was comprehensive
in its scope, public in its appeal, and scriptural in its method.
Under the title "Diwinyddiaeth y Cyfundeb" (The Denomination's Theology) it surveyed the baneful effects of the "advanced" theology from evolution to higher criticism, from
Hegel to F. D. Maurice, from *Lux Mundi* to T. K. Cheyne's
Bible Dictionary. Positively, Cynddylan Jones emphasised
the essentially supernatural quality of Christianity. "We
believe in God as a supernatural Being . . . in the Bible as
a supernatural revelation . . . in the supernatural in Christ."
Replying to the doubts cast on the historicity of the Pentateuch, for instance, he says, "No historic foundation for God's
appearance to Moses in the burning bush, or God's giving of
the Law on Sinai, or manna from heaven for food? And yet
Christ bases His arguments and preached sermons on these
very incidents."[12] His arguments rested on sound exposition
of the text of the Bible, were expressed in the traditional
framework of the Protestant confessions, and found their con-
firmation in the works of Calvin, John Owen, and Thomas
Goodwin. His substantiated conclusion was that the evolutionary end-product of higher criticism is stark unbelief.

The fruits of theological decline

There is ample evidence to show that this pernicious
influence had reached the churches. More serious perhaps was
the fact that the Sabbath Schools were troubled by it, the

subject under discussion at a Presbytery Sabbath School Convention in 1900 being "The Higher Criticism".[13] In June of that year a Welsh Presbyterian Moderator, Evan Phillips (later to be associated, through his son, John, with Evan Roberts the revivalist) had spoken, in an address on "Our Dangers and Needs", of the supreme need for revival :

"This is our great need; and all efforts to supply every other need will be in vain if this is not supplied . . . We do not know to what extent the conviction of the Church has deviated to this dangerous tendency of depending on human effort, but it is certain that there is a considerable body of error dragging it in an atheistic direction. The Hegelian philosophy, and evolutionary principles in their extreme form have flooded the realms of faith, with undoubtedly the most devastating effects . . . a spirit of error fills the air, so that a silent subconscious influence on the minds of men attracts them away from the living God, the personal God."

Writing retrospectively in March 1905 Phillips returned to the same theme to fill in some of the details :

"Did we not feel that atheism was making such a daring and overpowering attack on our land that it seemed nothing short of divine resources could withstand it? . . . Were not our intelligent young men, many of them, feasting on the poisonous dishes of Haeckel, Blatchford, etc? And had not doubtful, even atheistic, books been enthroned as objects of worship in the sacred precincts of our theological examinations?"[14]

The weekly paper of Welsh Presbyterianism, *Y Goleuad*, for 1st August 1900, carried the report of "an able and fair review" of *The Atonement in Modern Religious Thought*. Tacit approval was given to the book's insistence on the atonement having moral rather than substitutionary value. This was a flagrant betrayal of the denomination's Confession of Faith, and the paper was taken to task over it by a correspondent a fortnight later.

The same denomination's monthly periodical, *Y Drysorfa*, included in its November 1902 issue an article on "The need in Wales for a religious revival". Having noted the spiritual declension in the churches, and the thirst of the people "no longer for what edifies but what entertains", the author complained :

"English literature of a certain kind disseminates questionable and atheistic ideas among our people on every hand, and it is said that many already in our Sabbath Schools, especially in the towns, deny the inspiration, authority and infallibility of extensive portions of the Bible; the divinity of the Son's Person; the sacrifice and atonement of the cross; and the Person and work of the Holy Spirit. While the Church sleeps the enemy busily sows tares among the wheat, and nothing short of an outpouring of the Spirit from on high will uproot them and save our land from becoming a prey to atheism and ungodliness."

This concern for the active and healthy preservation of a doctrinal standard is found in an article in the same magazine for April 1904 : "The basic theology of our denomination : the importance of knowing it". Insistence is laid on the objective validity as well as the symbolic value of the Confession of Faith, and the writer laments the influx of "the most unbridled and extreme ideas from England and Germany". The seriousness of the situation, however, lay in the fact that "the haziest hypotheses are presented as truths which cannot possibly be shaken". The sheer intoxication of a new theology which championed so loudly a release from the trammels of traditional orthodoxy blinded many to its utter contingency. Liberal theology was not merely taking away the decorative appurtenances of Christianity, it was demolishing its very foundations.

The spiritual bankruptcy of the churches, thus deprived of the very cause and meaning of their existence, was the subject of many complaints before the revival broke out. Under the title, "The spiritual state of the churches", a correspondent to the *Goleuad* at the turn of the century (3rd January 1900) spoke of low attendances at Sunday services, fellowship and prayer meetings, of a decline in Bible reading and family worship. The remedy proposed was a penitent and humble pleading with God for another divine visitation in revival throughout the land. People were turning away from solid preaching and praying, and seeking the church more as a social meeting-place for the purpose of enjoyment. Bazaars, operettas, and similar events for raising funds were on the increase, while the spiritual appetite was becoming blunted and atrophied.[15] The Established Church in Wales complained of religious indifference, "one of the chief sins of the time", as being general throughout the land, and due to sheer lack of zeal.[16] There was a distinct falling away in church membership, too, during the last decade of the nineteenth century. An example of this was a report given at the North Wales Association of the Presbyterian Church of Wales in the spring of 1900, where a total loss of 12,844 was reported for that period, a figure which cannot be wholly accounted for by rural depopulation and the drift to Liverpool.[17]

Evidences of concern

In spite of this widespread defection in quantity and quality, there were many factors in the religious background of the revival which reflect some measure of concern and

longing for the prosperity of true religion. Past revivals were
constantly kept before the eyes of the common people in
published biographies and histories. The last two decades of
the nineteenth century especially witnessed the appearance
of a number of works dealing with the Welsh Calvinistic
Methodist "fathers", from William Hughes's *Life and Letters
of the Rev. Thomas Charles of Bala* (1881), to the more
extensive two-volume work *Y Tadau Methodistaidd* (1895,
1897; "The Calvinistic Methodist Fathers"). In between
these dates there appeared works on Howel Harris, Daniel
Rowland, William Williams, John Elias, Thomas Jones,
Roberts (Clynnog), and by 1897 a third edition of *Cofiant Y
Parch, Richard Owen,* the biography of the Welsh revivalist
greatly used of God in the early 1880s. A year later Edward
Parry's brief survey of Welsh revivals appeared under the
title *Llawlyfr ar Hanes y Diwygiadau Crefyddol yng Nghymru*
(Handbook on the History of Religious Revivals in Wales). It
included a chapter on "the latest awakenings" between 1886
and 1892. Such books kept the mighty works of God before
the churches, and were conducive to creating a desire that
similar activities on the part of the Holy Spirit should be
renewed.

This desire often found concrete and insistent expression
in the religious periodicals of the day. Sometimes they took
the form of articles calling for earnest prayer, at other times
they gave reports of discussions on the theme in various church
courts. Examples of the former have already been given, and
the most notable in the light of subsequent events was that of
the godly Dean David Howell, which appeared in the December 1902 issue of *Y Cyfaill Eglwysig,* a month before his
death.[18]

"The preaching, it is said, is able, scholarly, interesting, and instructive; it is however accompanied with but little unction and anointing—there is no smiting of the conscience, no laying bare the condition of the soul as in times past. The terminology of former ages, such as conviction, conversion, repentance, adoption, mortification of sin, self-loathing, and such like, has become to a great extent foreign and meaningless . . . The authority of the Bible and the fundamental truths of Christianity are being weighed in the balance of reason and criticism, as though they were nothing more than human opinions. A steadfast faith in the invisible, the miraculous, and the supernatural is regarded as open to question . . . But what of the remedy? . . . A Holy Spirit religion is the only cure for the moral and spiritual disease of Wales at this time . . . Take note : if it were known that this was my last message to my fellow-countrymen throughout the length and breadth of Wales, before being summoned to judgment, the light of eternity already breaking over me, it would be, that the principal need of my country and dear nation at present is still spiritual revival through a special outpouring of the Holy Spirit."

Dean Howell was not alone in his sentiments. The Congregational weekly, *Y Tyst*, carried five articles between 21st September and 19th October, 1904, on 'recent revivals'. These were based on answers supplied by various ministers to a questionnaire on the subject. The anonymous author's conclusions were :

1. That prayer has a prominent place in each awakening.

2. That there was considerable variety both in the motives which urged churches to pray for the Lord's visitation and also in the manner in which God worked in their midst.

3. That the ministers and churches must depend largely on local efforts.

4. That there are dangers as well as advantages in these awakenings.

In conclusion, the purpose of the articles was stated to be "the encouragement of ministers and churches to make strenuous efforts to secure God's richest blessing".[19] There were others disturbed with the theological fashion and wide-spread declension of the age.

The same matter received public airing in various representative gatherings. The Carmarthenshire Presbytery urged that the week of prayer in January, 1900, should be earnestly concerned with 'a more extensive outpouring of the Holy Spirit'. In North Wales, too, the same urgency was emphasised in several presbyteries, in April, 1900, at Caernarvonshire, and in the same year at the Conway Valley Presbytery; in November, 1901, the subject before the West Merionethshire Presbytery was 'The need for the Lord to come and work in an evident way' based on Psalm 119 : 126, 'It is time for thee, Lord, to work : for they have made void thy law'. The following year this concern found expression among the Welsh Established Church in a conference at Llangynwyd, Glamorganshire, dealing with 'The declension in religion and the need for revival'.[20] Apart from such collective evidences there were those who longed for a personal as well as a national quickening, and were equally convinced of the necessity for divine intervention to realize them. By their patient waiting on God they showed where their confidence lay, and they could not be dissuaded. In the gloomiest night God's stars shine all the more brightly, and it is 'when the enemy shall come in like a flood' that 'the Spirit of the Lord shall lift up a standard against him' (Isaiah 59 : 19). Even before 1904 God had lifted up His standard.

CHAPTER 4

CARDIGANSHIRE VILLAGE

BLAENANNERCH is a small straggling village some five miles north of the county town of Cardigan, thoroughly Welsh and quietly unpretentious. Its claim to fame is based exclusively on the remarkable scenes witnessed there in the autumn of 1904. The events which mark it off from the neighbouring scattered villages along the nearby Western seaboard belong to sacred rather than secular history. They took place in the simple, unadorned church of the Calvinistic Methodists, and brought together three men with whom God had been dealing in different ways. Unforeseen and un-rehearsed, the events of that day were marked forever on their souls, and became the proud spiritual heritage of a whole nation. Chiefly, however, it was the awful sense of God's presence in their midst which overwhelmed them, an experience of such shattering proportions that one of them, at least, was never quite the same afterwards.

Seth Joshua

The first of these men, Seth Joshua, has already been mentioned. Having joined the Forward Movement in 1891 he had been ordained two years later and had been in the vanguard of the work ever since. From Cardiff he removed to Newport to storm the enemy camp there. Back again in Cardiff at the turn of the century his labours were richly blessed. Some years' work in Swansea followed, and at the beginning of 1904 he was on a roving commission as denominational evangelist, holding one series of meetings after another in the growing centres of population in North and South Wales.

On the invitation of William Ross he conducted a fortnight's mission at Cowcaddens, Glasgow, at the end of January 1904, and reaped a rich spiritual harvest of souls. Here he saw the benefit of having trained workers in the church : "January, 25th. We had another great day today, and in the evening meeting fourteen souls sought the Saviour. It is a very pleasant sight to see so many workers able to lead seeking souls to Jesus. There is one worker to each seeker, and they never leave a soul to slip away, until the light of salvation breaks on the poor seeker. Glory be to God." At the end of the mission he could record in the same diary : "Tonight we had a remarkable time . . . The body of the church was full. I spoke on Isaiah chapter 62 verse 10, 'Go through, go through the gates,' that is, conviction, pardon, consecration, crucifixion, pentecost, abiding joy, service. Step by step the whole congregation seemed to go through into these experiences, some into the one, and some into the other of them. It was a fitting finish to a great mission."

Mission followed mission in his packed schedule, not without much spiritual conflict in some of them. At Llanhilleth in April, for example, he found the people holding out "with stubborn determination. I cannot remember seeing such resistance to God's power". Consequently when some were converted it was only "after much agony of soul on their behalf". Such occasions were not isolated, and proved his faith more than once. Of the mission at Prestatyn in May he had to confess "all the week I have toiled without seeing any fruit until tonight. My faith was tried, my heart began to fear. But tonight four young men and one young woman boldly confessed Christ. God be praised. I am ashamed and humbled. If not at the first three watches, He comes at the fourth".

Travelling so much of the time on his missionary labours left him little enough time for meditation, and this was a loss which he felt keenly. Following one of these rare occasions of intermission and quiet in a Cardiff public park he wrote: "I enjoyed a blessed time of reading and prayer . . . this day under a tree. Being wet, there were no people to disturb my meditations. From experience I find that freedom in prayer and readiness of matter largely depends upon Bible study. Communion with the written Word seems to be a staircase up to communion with the living Word." He was able to enjoy two more days of waiting upon God, days filled with unprecedented thoughts regarding the months ahead: "I am filled with a feeling that a change is soon coming over my future arrangements. There is a sense of unrest and foreboding . . . I am in a current. It is new, and goes in a direction hitherto unknown to me. I am drifting out into some unknown sea. Great Pilot, wilt Thou not pilot me past the rocks into my desired haven?" In the light of subsequent events it is hard not to regard these sentiments as prophetic.

Shortly afterwards he left for London where he talked with F. B. Meyer, "over some future plans connected with the Lord's work". Early in August his mission work was interrupted for a holiday at Llandrindod with many other Forward Movement workers. It was not exclusively a time of relaxation, for they attended the convention on Keswick lines as well as taking part in their own Forward Movement meetings. From the point of view of one of its organisers, Jessie Penn-Lewis, the convention was eminently successful:

"The conference bore upon it the marks of Spirit-born preparations . . . And again it was the message of the Cross, showing the experimental aspect of the Holy Spirit's work in the believer, the putting away of all known sin, deliverance through *identification with Christ in His death*, and the definite reception of the Holy Ghost as a necessity for all in the service of God. This was carried home to hearts by the power of God in such intensity that on the last two days it was manifest to all that the Spirit of God had come down in pentecostal power."[1]

Joshua, however, had serious misgivings about the emphases of the Convention. It was inevitable that a man whose soul was ablaze with a passion for aggressive evangelism should feel that this scriptural vision was lacking from the distinctively personal note of Keswick. "My one fear", he writes, "is that many people are in danger of cultivating holiness at the expense of service. It would be a thousand pities to see people make holiness a substitute for work."

He was aware, too, of another danger, and this related to the Keswick pattern for blessing : "I am bound to record what appears to me another danger in connection with the teaching I heard. Not with the doctrine, but the manner in which people were invited to reach the experience. I consider it a dangerous thing to become too dogmatic with regard to the steps leading into the blessing of spiritual fulness. My opinion is that this land of milk and honey is reached by many separate paths, and that the Holy Spirit leads into this in His own way. The theory sounds right when you listen to it, but each soul must go onward in his own way. Preach the Truth and leave it to God's Spirit".[2] Although he found some of the addresses "very searching indeed", as he had at the first convention the previous year, Keswick teaching made no lasting impression upon him and its influence upon his experience was of no consequence.

Vastly more important to his spiritual development and ministry was his communion with God. It was this intimate sustained fellowship which brought him a personal assurance of salvation; it gave him the compelling vision of militant evangelism and, above all, through it he was brought into a deeper realization of the Holy Spirit's provision of power in the service of God's kingdom. The nature of his dramatic conversion experience, the example of the Salvation Army's fiery zeal, the thoughtful reading of Puritan theology, each helped to frame the mould in which his Christian character was cast. His forthrightness was matched with studiousness. A memorable example of the former of these qualities is supplied by his wife : "One day he turned to me, and asked, 'Mary, are you saved?' Surprised at such a question I said, 'Well, you know, Seth, that I have been confirmed'. 'Yes, my dear,' he added, 'and vaccinated; but are you saved?' "

Instances of his studiousness are found in his diary at a very early period in his spiritual pilgrimage : "Rose at six this morning and enjoyed reading Luke chapter 1 and Richard Sibbes' *Bruised Reed*". "Went to Cardiff Exhibition and bought books, *History of the Puritans* and Manton". "Much blessed in reading Owen on 'Communion with Christ' ".

In an annual letter read to the churches in the first Sunday of 1899 Principal T. Charles Edwards had crystallized the distinctive contribution of the Forward Movement evangelists. He spoke of "the insistence on the necessity of the full assurance of faith", and "a second baptism as the second stage in the spiritual development", a work of the Holy Spirit invariably linked with any powerful and effective preaching of the gospel. Seth Joshua was one of these evangelists and, following his mission at Neath, he travelled to Cardiganshire on 17th September for the unexpectedly eventful meeting with the other two men at Blaenannerch.

Joseph Jenkins

The second man was Joseph Jenkins, minister of the Calvinistic Methodist cause at New Quay in his native Cardiganshire. Born in the heat of the 1859 revival he was brought up on a staple diet of prayer and the *Confession of Faith*. In his early teens he was apprenticed to a godly tailor in the Rhondda, and before starting to preach at twenty, he had come under strong evangelical impressions. Having been spiritually awakened under the preaching of the gospel (he particularly mentions a sermon on Lamentations 3 :27 'It is good for a man that he bear the yoke in his youth'), he was gripped by the evangelistic fervour of the Salvation Army. At that time the whole of the mining valley had been stirred by the impact of the Army's massive campaign against the religious and moral problems of that decadent society. It was an experience which he never forgot.

Having satisfied the denominational requirements for ordination, he was called to a charge in Caerphilly. With the help of John Pugh he commenced a weekly open-air ministry and under the blessing of God reaped a rich harvest. He removed to New Quay in 1892 after serving for three years in Liverpool. Two years later he found spiritual companionship with his nephew John Thickens who had received a call to nearby Aberaeron. Temperamentally, the two men were different. Jenkins was erratic and at times severe, while Thickens was more balanced and studious; but spiritually they were agreed in a common desire for more evidences of God's presence and power. The churches of the presbytery in which they served still benefited from the leadership of men who had been influenced by the 1859 revival, interest and activity in the Sunday School being especially prominent.

On the other hand the two men were disturbed by the

evidences of spiritual decline in the churches at the turn of the century. "It was agreed that we were on the verge of losing all spiritual fervour from our churches and that it would be entirely lost unless they were soon revived by the Spirit of Christ; that we would nurture sons and daughters who knew not the way of life in Christ; and that within a few years we would be deprived of those who had experienced the mighty things of the gospel. We feared that our people were looking to the County Council, the District Council, the Parish Council, and the Central Schools, which were new in our midst, to bring in a social Utopia; and that we would degenerate into lukewarmness in the work of the Lord."[3]

There was another, equally urgent, need. This was the need they felt in their own hearts and ministries, and Thickens wrote poignantly of their state at that time :

"We mourned together and, sometimes, we rejoiced together. The outlook of our little worlds was black, and one night we agreed that we were two evil spirits on account of our gross unfaithfulness to the Crucified, and we almost resolved to flee from the presence of the Lord to some Tarshish because our hearts were so black. He (Jenkins) would have overwhelming visions of the glory of the Gospel on occasions when his soul would humbly submit, but the cloud invariably returned. We know of hardly anything but a desolate darkness of soul. Both of us longed for the day of perpetual brilliance, but our longing was our only capital."

Jenkins was also troubled about the content of his preaching. He feared that its ethical rather than evangelical content at that period in his ministry disqualified him from seeing the success he desired. His preaching had been directed at the manifest hypocrisy of those who 'prayed by the yard and lied by the mile'. Then he remembered the Salvation Army's unwavering policy during those early years in the Rhondda. In the face of drunkenness, gambling, swearing and their accompanying evils the Army had avoided a frontal attack on these vices in a negative way, and had simply presented the Saviour who was "able to save to the uttermost".

Faced with this dilemma the two ministers stumbled on the Keswick teaching. In 1903 one of them heard a minister relate the blessings which he had received at Keswick. He was further helped in his distress by W. W. Lewis "who had yielded himself to Christ the Lord". Lewis, a Calvinistic Methodist minister at Carmarthen, had been liberal in his views of the Bible, but his life and ministry had been transformed, as well as his theological views changed, by an experience of the deep things of God about that time. Already he was being widely used in small conferences as he expounded the Word of God, and the two men must have looked upon him as one who could lead them to the spiritual oasis which had hitherto been only a mirage on the horizon of their thirst for God.

It was with these things in mind that Jenkins proposed to the presbytery that "means should be adopted to nurture devotion to the denomination and to Christ". The committee constituted to consider the matter had some difficulty in understanding his intentions. Many of them thought in terms of another 1859 revival, while Jenkins and Thickens desired a series of conferences on the theme of deepening the spiritual life in order to meet the need they felt in their own hearts and in the churches. They were thinking solely in Keswick categories. It was pointed out that a number of young men and women had been meeting since October for this very purpose in Thickens' church, and were making definite progress. On this basis it was agreed to hold such a conference, to which all the churches should appoint representatives, with W. W. Lewis, John M. Saunders and his wife as speakers. This was to be the first of five held in south Cardiganshire during 1904, and other speakers included W. S. Jones, E. Keri Evans, and Seth Joshua.

Jenkins was burdened with the spiritual needs of the youth of his church and arranged to meet them after the Sunday morning service. Apart from this he would spend hours at night in prayer for them. While reading Andrew Murray's *With Christ in the School of Prayer* he felt convicted of not having fulfilled his ministry, and a book on Moody intensified this sense of guilt. He prayed as never before, and one night in particular he lost all sense of time. Having laid hold upon God he continued to wrestle until a blessing was received which equipped him with power from on high. Getting up from his knees he became aware of a blue flame which almost enshrouded him rhythmically off and on for some time. It was an experience he never forgot and could only take as being a visible sign of the intense spiritual communion which he had enjoyed with God.

The first conference, held in New Quay over the New Year, was attended by about fifty from the various churches. Saunders spoke on "Assurance" and Lewis on "The Achan in our lives". In addition, the sacrament of the Lord's Supper was administered, Saunders preached on John 3 : 3 ("Except a man be born again, he cannot see the kingdom of God"), his wife urged an experience of Christ, and Lewis spoke on "Yield yourselves unto God" (Romans 6 : 13). A testimony meeting on the second afternoon brought the conference to an end. Thickens wrote later : "The testimony meeting was the most powerful I have ever attended . . . There was no note of jubilation in the meetings; indeed, we sang but little, because it was a time of heart-searching, and the chief effect was to create within us an intense longing to know Christ's love, a desire that God in Christ should satisfy us with something—something which we could not define, and the experience of many in the days which followed was 'I stretch forth my hands unto thee : my soul thirsteth after thee, as a thirsty land' (Psalm 143 :6)".

Nearly two months later Jenkins was preaching on I John 5 :4, "this is the victory that overcometh the world, even our faith" at the Sunday evening service. One young woman named Florrie Evans, under an overwhelming sense of compulsion, followed him home and after considerable trepidation ventured to the door. Quite overcome by her fears of being under the domination of the world, she longed for peace and joy. Jenkins advised her to acknowledge the Lordship of Christ over her life, and that in the solitude of her own home she should submit to the leading of the Holy Spirit.

The following Sunday morning the young people's after-meeting was held as usual, with about sixty present. When the prepared papers had been read, Jenkins called upon anyone present to relate their spiritual experience in a few words. A few moments' silence ensued, and then Florrie Evans rose to say, "I love the Lord Jesus with all my heart". The effect was startling, and an overpowering sense of God's presence seemed to solemnize and yet excite the whole congregation. The young people's meetings were subsequently attended with the most heavenly influences, two more young women having been set ablaze, Maud Davies and May Phillips. Several visits were made by the young people to neighbouring churches to share the blessing, and the second conference soon followed. It was held at Aberaeron on June 30th and July 1st, and although it enjoyed the divine unction the blessing was local and personal.

When Seth Joshua arrived at New Quay in September he found "a remarkable revival spirit" there. He was able to report on the first Sunday's ministry (18th September), "I have

never seen the power of the Holy Spirit so powerfully manifested among the people as at this place just now . . . It was
easy to preach today".

The ensuing week's meetings for Joshua at New Quay were
full of intense activity. There seemed to be no satisfying of
the spiritual appetite of the people, and the powerful influences kept him from his bed until the early hours of the
morning. People had become oblivious of time and physical
needs such as food or sleep. Never was Joshua's diary filled
with more inspiring entries :

19th Monday. The revival is breaking out here in greater
power. Many souls are receiving full assurance of salvation.
The spirit of prayer and of testimony is falling in a marvellous manner. The young are receiving the greatest measure
of blessing. They break out into prayer, praise, testimony and
exhortation in a wonderful way.
20th. The revival goes on. I cannot leave the building . . .
until 12 and even 1 o'clock in the morning—I have closed the
service several times and yet it would break out again quite
beyond the control of human power.
21st. Yes several souls—that is all I can say. I don't know
the number, and they are not drunkards or open sinners, but
they are members of the visible church not grafted into the
true vine, that is, not joined unto the Lord, not baptized into
one Spirit. They are entering into full assurance of faith
coupled with a baptism of the Holy Spirit. The joy is intense.
22nd. We held another remarkable meeting to-night. Group
after group came out to the front seeking the full assurance of
faith. What was wonderful to me was the fact that every
person engaged in prayer, without one exception. The tongue
of fire came upon each. We lost all sense of time in this
service.

23rd. I am of the opinion that forty conversions took place this week. It is as near as I can fix it. I also think that those seeking assurance may be fairly counted as converts, for they had never received Jesus as a personal Saviour before . . . I shall thank God for this blessed time to my own soul. I am saturated, melted and made soft as willing clay in the hands of a potter.

At Newcastle Emlyn

So ended the week's unparalleled services, and after less than four hours' sleep that night Joshua was on the way to his next mission, the venue being Newcastle Emlyn. According to reports he had received, the church was distinctly Laodicean in its lukewarmness and inhospitality to the risen Lord.

September was the month when the students returned to the preparatory school at Newcastle Emlyn under John Phillips. Among them was a young man who would later play an important part in the revival alongside its leading figure. Sidney Evans' early religious experience had been gained mainly in the Sunday School and church fellowship meetings. The family had moved to Gorseinon, near Swansea, when he was eight years old; his mother, a godly, thrifty woman, but the father of the large family an avowed unbeliever. The latter was to be gloriously converted in the early days of the revival, after much prayer on his behalf and considerable struggle in his own soul.

After a period of apprenticeship in a grocer's shop Evans felt constrained to offer himself as a candidate for the ministry of the Calvinistic Methodists. Eventually he found his way to the preparatory school, and, with many of the other students, to Joshua's meetings. It was at one of these meetings that he faced a spiritual crisis which changed his whole life and determined his future ministry.

According to Joshua progress was slow : "*25th (Sunday)*. I tried to give them an account of the revival at New Quay when in the pulpit this morning, but I broke down under the emotion resting on my spirit. Many others wept in the chapel and there are signs here of a deep desire. I preached four times this day; nothing has moved yet.

26th. There was a touch of power in the service to-night, and a few moved towards the cross. I find scarcely a soul here in the joy of assurance. It is a pitiable sight to me. When I tested the meeting only a small handful among hundreds would stand up to confess a present salvation. The witness of the church is nothing in this state.

27th. A large number were blessed this evening. Some students received blessing and confessed salvation. The Lord will certainly move this place. The yearning is here among the people."

Even though the next day, Wednesday, was the first day of the Blaenannerch conference Joshua recorded in his diary that he received support from several of the New Quay young people : "About 15 young people from New Quay came all the way to Newcastle Emlyn today. I did not preach but allowed them to speak, pray, sing and exhort as the Holy Spirit led them. The fire burned all before it. Souls were melted and many cried out for salvation. Praise the Lord for this service. Many knelt in their seats, but I cannot say what the number was. The Master knows." Although others of the young people had left for Blaenannerch that day, Evan Roberts in their midst, Sidney Evans seems to have remained at the Newcastle Emlyn meetings. For him it was to be a day of great things.

He had been under sore conviction for some time. The question which gave him no peace and seared his conscience became more and more insistent during the last week-end of

that month : "I preach Christ as Saviour—do I know Him
thus myself?" Although he felt compelled to pray at
Joshua's meetings, and had been urged by Maud Davies and
Florrie Evans of New Quay to make open confession of Christ,
it was only after a severe conflict that he submitted at the
Wednesday night meeting :

"The devil argued with me, 'Don't be so foolish as to show
all these people that it is only now you are giving yourself to
Christ. They all know about you, that you preach'. But
having decided to confess Christ I felt better. On Wednesday
night after praying in the first meeting I found a little relief.
In the second meeting I was constrained to pray again, so
down I went on my knees, and prayed that God would save
me and take full control of my life . . . I could no longer
restrain myself or remain on my knees . . . I got up on my
feet shouting 'I love Jesus Christ, and give myself entirely
to Him . . .'. I felt all was well; the light had come, and I
was as happy as the day is long . . . There was no sleep that
night with the sheer joy and anticipation of going to Blaenannerch the following morning."[4]

In the providence of God all things were now ready for the
spiritual drama of the next day. Jenkins was already on the
scene and the others would travel from Newcastle Emlyn in
the early morning. It was to be "the day of God's power",
and His people would be willing (Psalm 110 :3). On that day
God was to open a fountain of general and national blessing.

CHAPTER 5

SPIRITUAL FERMENT

Evan Roberts

THE third man involved in that crucial conference was Evan John Roberts. Formerly a miner and blacksmith, he was by that time an accredited candidate for the Calvinistic Methodist ministry of a mere one month's standing, and in the twenty-sixth year of his life. At the turn of the century Seth Joshua had felt the danger of the prevailing emphasis upon educational rather than spiritual attainments, and after a "very heated discussion over the intellectual qualifications for the pulpit", he "had it laid upon his heart to pray God to go and take a lad from the coal-mine or from the field, even as He took Elisha from the plough, to revive His work". Not only was his prayer answered, but he was to witness the divine mantle fall on God's chosen instrument that very day.

Born in Loughor, on the Glamorgan and Carmarthenshire border, the main influences upon his early life were the Bible, the Sunday School, and family worship. Before he was twelve he had started working with his father in the coalmine, and in little over a year he had been accepted as a communicant at Moriah, the Calvinistic Methodist church where the family worshipped. About that time he was challenged by something that was spoken in the fellowship meeting, the Welsh 'seiat', by one of the elders : "Remember to be faithful. What if the Spirit descended and you absent? Remember Thomas! What a loss he had!" From that moment Roberts resolved to pray for the Spirit and to be faithful in the means of grace :

63

"I said to myself: 'I will have the Spirit'. And through all weather, and in spite of all difficulties, I went to the meetings . . . Prayer meeting Monday evening at the chapel; prayer meeting Tuesday evening at Pisgah (Sunday School branch); Church meeting Wednesday evening; Band of Hope Thursday; class Friday evening . . . For ten or eleven years I have prayed for a revival. I could sit up all night to read or talk about revivals. It was the Spirit that moved me to think about a revival."[1]

He was seldom without his Bible. Even underground he would often refer to a copy which, apart from a few torn and scorched leaves, survived a pit explosion when five miners were killed. An eager thirst for knowledge was assuaged by reading such books as Bunyan's *Pilgrim's Progress,* A. A. Hodge's *Outlines of Theology,* and Thomas Charles' *Geiriadur Ysgrythurol (Scripture Dictionary).* The latter's *Hyffordd-wr yn Egwyddorion y Grefydd Gristionogol (The Christian Instructor: or Catechism on the Principles of the Christian Religion)* was especially prized in Calvinistic Methodist circles, and Roberts' spiritual appetite was often satisfied with its rich biblical teaching.

Work at the collieries even in those early years was uncertain. He had to leave home on more than one occasion to find employment, when the local pit stopped because of a strike or for some other reason. Eventually, in 1902, he was apprenticed at a smithy, but for a number of years he had become increasingly aware of a constraint to preach. There could be only one outcome; to offer himself, even at the age of twenty-five, as candidate for the ministry. By the end of 1903 the decisive step had been taken. Writing to a friend, he explained his reasons for coming to this unavoidable conclusion:

"I have had more than enough of physical labour, while my soul thirsts for knowledge and a wider sphere of usefulness. I am older than most, but not too old, surely? There was a time in my life when I felt the urge strongly, but when I learned that the influence of the 'schools' shattered the spirit of ministerial students, I had no more spirit left in me to venture among them. Now I see no other possible avenues to the pulpit. Like others I am resolved to walk the same path . . . It is reasonable for you to ask what causes me to take this step . . . On examination I find the following motives constrain me : (1) The passionate longing of my soul for ten years which I cannot quench . . . (2) The voice of the people of God . . . (3) God's infinite love together with the promise of the Holy Spirit. Last Sunday night while thinking about the greatness of the work and the danger of my dishonouring God, I could not but weep. And I prayed that the Lord should baptize you and me with the Holy Spirit."[2]

The months which followed this decision were taken up with applying himself to preaching probationary sermons and sitting Scripture examinations to satisfy the denominational requirements.

It was not exclusively a time of intellectual preparation. The spiritual exercises of prayer, Bible reading and meditation maintained his communion with God. In the spring of 1904 he entered into an experience of such close communion with God that it seemed to remove him out of the body into a third heaven, and the white heat of this intimate fellowship remained with him for several months.

"One Friday night last spring, when praying by my bedside before retiring, I was taken up to a great expanse— without time and space. It was communion with God.

Before this I had a far-off God. I was frightened that night, but never since. So great was my shivering that I rocked the bed, and my brother, being awakened, took hold of me thinking I was ill. After that experience I was awakened every night a little after one o'clock. This was most strange, for through the years I slept like a rock, and no disturbance in my room would awaken me. From that hour I was taken up into the divine fellowship for about four hours. What it was I cannot tell you, except that it was divine. About five o'clock I was again allowed to sleep on till about nine. At this time I was again taken up into the same experience as in the earlier hours of the morning until about twelve or one o'clock . . . This went on for about three months."[3]

A similar visitation of the Holy Spirit was experienced by David Morgan, the Welsh revivalist of 1859, immediately before he commenced his revival activities.

"Not yet had he received power from on high, and as he hurried home to the united prayer meeting . . . his bosom was agitated by intense and conflicting emotions. Though he had sought the blessing for years, he was abashed when he realized that it was at hand, awaiting his acceptance. He retired to rest at his usual time on Tuesday evening, and slept for some hours. He awoke about 4 a.m., and was instantly conscious that some strange, mysterious change had come over him. He was aware with awe of a marvellous illumination of his faculties, especially of his memory. 'I awoke about four in the morning', said he himself, 'remembering everything of a religious nature that I had ever learnt or heard'."[4]

Over a century previously, at the commencement of the evangelical awakening, one of the Welsh reformers, Howel

Harris, had proved the same degree of nearness to God in the solitude of Llangasty church shortly after his conversion. He carefully recorded it in his diary :

"June 18th, 1735, being in secret prayer, I felt suddenly my heart melting within me, like wax before the fire, with love to God my Saviour. I felt not only love and peace, but also a *longing* to be dissolved and to be with Christ; and there was a cry in my inmost soul, with which I was totally un-acquainted before, it was this—*Abba, Father; Abba Father!* I could not help calling God *my* Father; I knew that I was his child, and that he loved me; my soul being filled and satiated, crying, 'It is enough—I am satisfied; give me strength, and I will follow thee through fire and water'. I could now say that I was happy indeed. There was in me 'a well of water springing up into everlasting life'; yea, 'the love of God was shed abroad in my heart by the Holy Ghost'. —John chapter 4, verse 14, Romans chapter 5, verse 5."[5]

The inexpressible comfort which he felt in his soul and the sense of God's presence which he enjoyed daily were such that he "could talk of nothing but spiritual things".

In each case this unforgettable experience was evidently an activity of the Holy Spirit, related to, but not part of, His ordinary working in sanctification.

By the middle of September the time had come for Evan Roberts to leave Loughor for the preparatory school at New-castle Emlyn. The move was made with much trepidation and the outcome was inevitable : "When I went to school . . . Oh! I was afraid that I would lose the communion. I had set aside half an hour daily for it. And for the first week I did the school work very well. But after that all the time was taken up. I had four days in bed with a severe cold, but day and night there was nothing but prayer. The last night of the four I was bathed in perspiration—the result of the cold and of communion with God".[8]

Blessing at Blaenannerch

Although Roberts was recovering from the cold he was unable to attend Joshua's meetings until Tuesday night. However, he heard reports of the Monday meeting from Sidney Evans. The young women from New Quay had spoken at a youth meeting, and when Joshua emphasized the importance of submission and utter self-denial in the service which followed, Evans had felt God's presence filling the place. On the Wednesday Joshua laboured at Newcastle Emlyn while Roberts and others of the young people travelled to Blaenannerch for the first of the two days' conference arranged by Jenkins and Thickens.

The two ministers had been apprehensive of the effect of the summer break on the conference. Saunders was unable to come, but Joshua was available for the second day. Even though Roberts does not seem to have felt much on the Wednesday apart from a patient "waiting for the fire to fall", he could say, "the altar is built, the wood in place, the offering ready". Thickens on the other hand had never felt such unction on the ministry of W. W. Lewis, who preached on Philippians 2 : 15, 'shine as lights in the world' : "This mighty man of God was clothed with power from on high, and we were summoned to a scrupulous assize . . . each one became a terror unto himself. We saw ourselves in the light of the last judgment".

It was at half-past nine the following morning that the fire fell on Roberts' offering. Joshua recorded in his diary, "grand meetings today at Blaenannerch and many cried for mercy. It was a remarkable thing to hear one young man". They had started from Newcastle Emlyn early that day with about twenty others, singing hymns on the way. They arrived in time for the 7 a.m. meeting of open discussion, at which W. W. Lewis took the leading part. Before breaking off for breakfast, Joshua's prayer made an explosive impression on Roberts' mind : "At the close the Rev. Seth Joshua prayed, and said, during his prayer, 'Lord, do this, and this, and this, etc., and bend us'. He did not say, 'O Lord, bend us'. It was the Spirit that put the emphasis for me on 'Bend us'. 'That is what you need', said the Spirit to me. And as I went out I prayed, O Lord, bend me".[7]

During breakfast the fact that he had refused some bread and butter because he was full, while another accepted it, was a parable of his need : "Is it possible that God is offering me the Spirit, and that I am unprepared to receive Him; that others are ready to receive, but are not offered? Now my bosom was quite full and tight".

Evan Roberts' spiritual excitement at the first meeting had not passed unnoticed. The two men mainly responsible for organizing the conference were seriously disturbed at this outward expression of agitation. They still looked on the conference as a quiet opportunity to deepen the spiritual life, a kind of Cardiganshire counterpart to Keswick. Thickens especially failed to see how this aim would be achieved in an atmosphere which had gone out of control spiritually. Once the meeting was allowed free expression, it would end in a spiritual ferment under the leadership of a spiritual neurotic such as the young Roberts. They were soon to see that the Spirit's dealings could not be contained or confined within a doctrinaire straitjacket, and, having seen, were constrained to acknowledge the sovereignty of the Holy Spirit, and were themselves used as His instruments in the same work.

When Roberts went into the 9 o'clock meeting he was conscious that he would have to pray. "As one and the other

prayed I put the question to the Spirit, 'Shall I pray now?'
'Wait a while', said He. When a few more had prayed I felt
a living power pervading my bosom. It took my breath
away, and my legs trembled exceedingly. This living power
became stronger and stronger as each one prayed, until I felt
it would tear me apart, and as each one finished I would ask
'May I pray now?' At last as someone stopped, I prayed.
My whole bosom was in turmoil, and if I had not prayed I
would have burst. What agitated my bosom? It was that
verse, 'God commendeth His love' (Romans 5 :8). I fell on
my knees with my arms over the seat in front of me, my face
was bathed in perspiration, and the tears flowed in streams, so
that I thought it must be blood gushing forth. Thereupon
Mrs. Davies of New Quay came to wipe my perspiration.
Mag. Phillips stood on my right, and Maud Davies on my
left. For about two minutes it was terrible. I cried out, 'Bend
me! Bend me! Bend us! Oh! Oh! Oh! Oh!' As she was
wiping my face Mrs. Davies said 'O! amazing grace!' 'Yes',
I echoed, 'O! amazing grace!' It was God's commending
His love which bent me, while I saw nothing in it to commend.
After I was bent, what a wave of peace flooded my bosom.
While I was in this state of jubilation the congregation sang
'I am coming, Lord, coming now to Thee'. Then the fearful
bending of the judgment day came to my mind, and I was
filled with compassion for those who must bend at the judgment, and I wept. Following that the salvation of the human
soul was solemnly impressed upon me. I felt ablaze with a
desire to go through the length and breadth of Wales to tell
of the Saviour; and had it been possible, I was willing to pay
God for doing so."[8]

Jenkins and Joshua returned to their spheres of ministry, one
to prepare for the next conference along the usual lines, the

other to prepare for the work of the Forward Movement. Both were eventually caught up in the work of the revival, and ministered in different parts of the country with considerable success. For Evan Roberts the days that followed were filled with the compelling need to win the Principality for Christ. The vision of God's love on that "most terrible and sublime day" of his life was not only compelling : it was inescapable.

The witness of the Spirit

With so much work to be done Roberts could not settle down to his studies, far less use any of his time for leisure. The following day he drew out a list of the young people who would constitute a team with which to visit the towns and villages of every county to preach the gospel. The names were those of the young women of New Quay, Sidney Evans and himself. Finance need be no problem, for inasmuch as he had offered up himself to God the £200 which he had saved would support, on his reckoning, ten workers for twenty-eight weeks. In spite of this careful assessment of their resources they found no liberty in finalising their arrangements.

The next few days they spent in Bible reading, prayer, and speaking in various places. The nights were interrupted by visions which spoke of the advance of Christ's kingdom on an unprecedented scale, and seasons of unfettered communion with God. Roberts recalled one night in particular :

"Sidney had gone to bed at 10 o'clock, and I sought to direct all my energies to the lessons. Suddenly, the thought came to my mind of a blessing for which I had not offered thanks. I immediately sought the throne of grace to give praise. Back again to my studies, but first I looked at the time—'how odd', I thought, 'it's 11 o'clock' . . . and tried to go over in my mind how I had lost a whole hour. I looked

again, and another hour had gone. I jumped to my feet, and
hastened to the bedroom. Sidney asked, 'What time is it?'
'Midnight', I answered. 'Were you able to press on?' 'Oh,
yes, but not with the Greek'."[9]

Those days were filled with joy and peace, in waiting upon
God and sharing the vision of 100,000 to be won for Christ.
Evan Phillips spoke of this period :

"Evan Roberts was like a particle of radium in our midst.
Its fire was consuming and felt abroad as something which
took away sleep, cleared the channels of tears, and sped the
golden wheels of prayer throughout the area . . . I did not
weep much in the 1859 revival, but I have wept now until my
heart is supple. In the midst of the greatest tearfulness I have
found the greatest joy. I had felt for a year or two that there
was a sighing of the wind, and something whispered that the
storm could not be far away. Soon I felt the waters begin to
cascade. Now the bed belongs to the river and Wales belongs
to Christ."[10]

The 100,000 would not be won without such weeping.

On the 10th of October Roberts began sharing the vision
by letter with his brother, Dan, at home in Loughor. Part of
it reads, "The wheels of the gospel chariot are to turn swiftly
before long, and it is a privilege to give a hand in the work.
I do not know whether you possess the joy of the Gospel . . .
but if you are to have it you must be willing to do the Spirit's
bidding . . . You must put yourself entirely at the Holy
Spirit's disposal".[11] Writing to another correspondent he
expressed his fears about having forgotten to pay a debt,
offered restitution, and gave an account of his spiritual experience at that time :

"Before I came to Newcastle Emlyn I thought it would be
hard to put aside the long hours of fellowship with God, but I

have been pleasantly surprised. If I found pleasure in the exercise before, I now have the purest joy upon earth. And oh! I cannot tell how happy I feel, because God is at work so powerfully in my life, and has been of late, especially so at Blaenannerch. We have come into contact with the young men and women of New Quay and the divine fire has taken hold of us . . . the devil is doing his worst these days. He attacks me with all his resources and also ploughs up my past life. But I rejoice that all is covered by the merit of the Blood . . . I have received three great blessings : 1. I have lost all nervousness. 2. I can now sing all day whereas before I was hindered by some physical impediment. 3. I had become as hard as flint even though, remember, the supreme desire and sole aim of my life was to serve God—but, praise be to God, at Blaenannerch I was bent low, so low that I had to cry out 'Praise Him!' How easy it is to give thanks now !"[12]

Something of his triumph was noticed especially in his prayers as he visited churches in the neighbourhood to supply the pulpit. Increasingly he came to see the importance of implicit and unqualified reliance on the personal influences of the Holy Spirit.

Already the emphases of his future revival ministry were emerging; obedience to the Holy Spirit's leading, confession and restitution, together with the full assurance of faith, the priority of prayer, and the pre-eminence of Christ in all things. An instance of his concern for the glory of God was the part he took in a meeting at another country church in Cardiganshire, Capel Drindod. A marked coldness was felt in the meeting on account of empty talk taking the place of prayer and praise. Roberts rose to his feet and with righteous indignation said that Christ was not being given His due honour because men were showing themselves too much. "With that, he seemed to collapse like a felled tree, and prayed in a manner never heard before in that congregation. What wonderful prayer! It burst through to the hearts and consciences of many, and Christ was glorified from that moment: it was an extraordinary meeting."[13] That night he failed to sleep. "The room was full of the Holy Spirit. The outpouring was so overpowering that I had to shout and plead with God to stay His hand."

Repeatedly during those days in late October 1904 he expressed concern for his home church at Loughor, especially for the young people. He knew well their fears, and reticence in prayer, their uncertainty regarding eternal issues and their ignorance of the Holy Spirit. They lacked peace, joy, assurance of forgiveness, and power. In a letter to his sister at the end of October he outlines the path of blessing: "First, you must *feel* that you are a *lost sinner*, then you must *feel* that Christ died for *you*, and lastly, you must have the baptism of the Holy Spirit, and then work."[14] On the last Sunday of that month the Holy Spirit laid Loughor on his heart with irresistible compulsion. He was unable to follow the sermon or join in the worship. There was an insistent voice which clamoured for his submission. The following morning he sent a note to Florrie Evans of New Quay advising her of his intention to hold meetings in Loughor and coveting the prayers of his friends: "I am this morning about to return home for a week among the young people. The reason for this is that the Holy Spirit wills it . . . I implore you in the name of our Lord Jesus to remember us especially at Moriah, Loughor. Meetings will be held every night for a week. Ask all the young people to remember us."

It had been difficult for him to leave Loughor for the school at Newcastle Emlyn, with the possibility of losing the precious time of communion with God weighing on his mind. His studies had already proved abortive in the face of the elevated spiritual experiences which were now his birthright. Blaenannerch had finally unsettled him as far as the school was concerned. Since that momentous day he had been learning in the school of the Spirit, and it was no theoretical knowledge which had been imparted to him. Already he had tasted the sweetness of applying the divine teaching to some churches in Cardiganshire, and his vision had been broadened to take in the entire sweep of the Principality.

Finally, the immediate sphere of the Spirit's operations, where he would impart that heavenly wisdom to men and women in their need, had been gradually but unmistakably revealed to him. The Spirit's choice was the scriptural pattern : "Ye shall receive power, after that the Holy Ghost is come upon you : and ye shall be witnesses unto me both in Jerusalem, and in all Judaea, and in Samaria, and unto the uttermost part of the earth" (Acts 1 :8). He was on the way home.

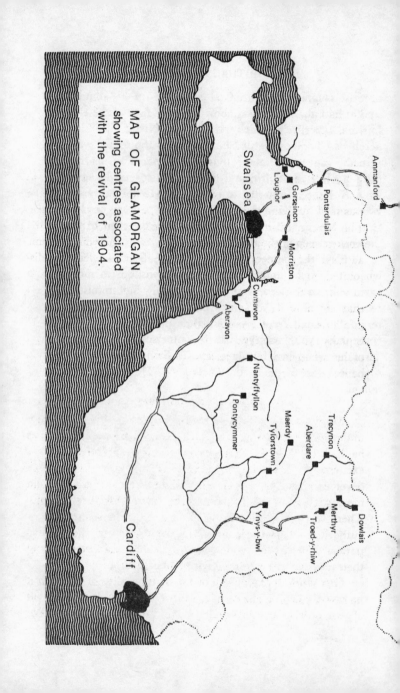

MAP OF GLAMORGAN
showing centres associated
with the revival of 1904.

Swansea

Loughor
Gorseinon
Morriston
Pontardulais
Amnanford

Cwmavon
Aberavon

Nantyffyllon
Pontycymmer
Maerdy
Tylorstown
Aberdare
Trecynon
Merthyr
Dowlais
Troed-y-rhiw
Ynys-y-bwl

Cardiff

CHAPTER 6

REVIVAL CENTRE

HARDLY had the train taking Evan Roberts home to Loughor left the station at Newcastle Emlyn before he was busy writing a letter. It was brief, factual, and in pencil. The burden of it was a request for prayer on behalf of the week of meetings he intended to hold with the young people at his home church, Moriah. The rest of the letter is disjointed, giving an impression of excitement and anticipation in view of the course events were taking. Both letters written that morning had carried one glowing message : the Spirit's infallible earnest of a bright prospect for the proposed venture.[1] Equally clear, however, had been the Spirit's disapproval of his scheme to take a team of young people with him. So he travelled alone.

"Your young men shall see visions"

Many factors accounted for his sudden return to Loughor under such circumstances. Chief among them were the visions he had received in that period of unprecedented religious excitement. His spiritual perception had been considerably developed and he could not fail to draw inspiration and motivation from those supernatural, extra-biblical revelations. There was no question in his mind as to their authenticity or authority. They were given in conformity to the biblical pattern (Joel 2 :28, "your young men shall see visions"), and their message was consistent with biblical truth.

One vision spoke to him of the awful reality of hell. In it he saw a yawning chasm in the form of a fiery, bottomless pit of vast proportions surrounded by an impenetrable wall. For those in the pit it was a place of torment, and all had entered by the solitary door. A voice spoke to him, "You too would be in their midst apart from God's grace". The mention of grace immediately changed the scene. He found himself with his back to the door, and coming down an incline towards him were countless numbers of people, a surging mass stretching away to the horizon with their faces set towards the pit. From sheer anguish of soul at the sight of this fearfully solemn tragedy enacted before him, he cried with fierce intensity upon God to rescue them. He pleaded that hell's door should be closed for one year so that they might have an opportunity to repent.[2] The impression left by this vision remained on his soul for a long time, and the revivalist often referred to it with the profoundest feeling in his public ministry, thankful to God for the respite provided by the revival to so many in answer to his prayer.

On another occasion the vision was concerned with Christ's victory over the devil. It came at a time when Roberts was despondent over the Church's impotence to reach the unconverted :

"For days he had been brooding over the apparent failure of modern Christian agencies; and he felt wounded in the spirit that the Church of God should so often be attacked. While in this 'Slough of Despond' he walked in the garden. It was about 4 p.m. Suddenly, in the hedge on his left, he saw a face full of scorn, hatred and derision, and heard a laugh as of defiance. It was the Prince of this world, who exulted in his despondency. Then there suddenly appeared another figure, gloriously arrayed in white, bearing in hand a flaming sword borne aloft. The sword fell athwart the first figure, and it instantly disappeared. He could not see the face of the Swordbearer."[3]

The message was immediately evident: the Church of Christ was to be triumphant. Here, then, lay the Holy Spirit's earnest, both clear and conclusive, stimulating his faith and soliciting his activity. When the flames of the revival were thoroughly kindled, he referred to it as being the vindication of his belief in the vision's validity and divinity. "Full of the promise which that vision conveyed", he would say, "I went to Loughor, and from Loughor to Aberdare, and from Aberdare to Pontycymmer. And what do I see? The promise literally fufilled. The sword is descending on all hands, and Satan is put to flight".[4]

A similiar message was conveyed in the visions he received of the moon. It appeared with greater brilliance than ever before, increasing in size and showing pulsating movements as he watched. In a matter of moments the moon seemed to reflect the divine presence and there appeared an arm out-stretched towards the world, claiming something for itself before being withdrawn.[5] At another time the arm and hand were indistinct, but the piece of paper which it held had the figures "100,000" written on it.[6] After that, whenever he prayed, he had no peace until he had asked God specifically for that number of souls.

Each vision was presented in biblical categories such as the victory of Christ's kingdom, the spiritual conflict with Satan, and the power of God in salvation. They were also prophetic in nature, because each found in the subsequent revival, which spread not only over Wales but also across the world, its literal and complete fulfilment. However, although their details were startling and their meaning unmistakable, Roberts dared not act until the way had become clear.

The vision that finally initiated his journey home was the hardest of all. In the light of it, lists of workers and their itineraries, mission teams and their financial arrangements were all of no avail for the moment. Sitting in the evening service on 30th October at Newcastle Emlyn, the clarion call of God's Spirit was for him alone, and it was irresistible. In an interview with W. T. Stead (himself a child of the 1859 revival), Roberts told the story of his struggle that night :

"I could not fix my mind upon the service, for always before my eyes I saw, as in a vision, the schoolroom in my own village. And there, sitting in rows before me, I saw my old companions and all the young people, and I saw myself addressing them. I shook my head impatiently, and strove to drive away this vision, but it always came back. And I heard a voice in my inward ear as plain as anything, saying, 'Go and speak to these people'. And for a long time I would not. But the pressure became greater and greater, and I could hear nothing of the sermon. Then at last I could resist no longer, and I said, 'Well, Lord, if it is Thy will, I will go'. Then instantly the vision vanished, and the whole chapel became filled with light so dazzling that I could faintly see the minister in the pulpit, and between him and me the glory as the light of the sun in heaven".[7]

Equipped though he had been with the divine promise of blessing and success, the prospect of entering upon this onerous task on his own must still have been terrifying. In Cardiganshire there had always been Sidney Evans, or Florrie Evans, or others to shoulder the burden with him; but to labour among his own people in what he knew to be an impossible situation would be an overwhelming trial of faith. Unknown and inexperienced, he could count on no "techniques of persuasion", no advertising or publicity campaigns, no mass media coverage. Humanly speaking, therefore, he was about to embark on a mistaken course which could only end in disaster, frustration and scandal. He was on his own

—with God, called to be one of that rare company in the annals of the faithful, a spiritual descendant of lonely men of God like Elijah, and Jeremiah, and John the Baptist.

"A prophet in his own country"

At home in Island House were his parents, his sisters Mary, Sarah and Catherine and his brother Dan. The reason Evan gave for his unexpected return from the school appeared to them unusual. His manner was suspicious, his claims extravagant and his questions seemed meaningless. They showed no little scepticism at his avowed intention of holding a week's meetings for the youth of the church. His excited laughter at the Spirit's guarantee of success in a promised revival, alternating with his uncontrolled weeping because of the spiritual burden of the country's need, made the others feel uncannily uncomfortable with fear for his mental stability. In addition, his talk of personal blessing, of being filled and baptized with the Holy Spirit, and similar subjects, baffled them completely, for what could they know of these things?

In 1904 the last day of October fell on a Monday. Its significance lay in the fact that the weekly prayer meeting at Moriah was held on that night. The other customary week-night meetings were the Tuesday prayer meeting at Pisgah (a branch of Moriah nearer the Roberts' home), and the Thursday church fellowship meeting—the Welsh "seiat"—at Moriah. The youth meetings would have to be specifically arranged by Roberts himself with the co-operation of the appropriate ministers, Daniel Jones of Moriah and Thomas Francis of the daughter church, Libanus, at nearby Gorseinon. They complied with his request, Jones on the Monday and Francis on the Wednesday. His interview with the latter was particularly noteworthy. "I intended staying only three or five minutes", Roberts wrote a few days later, "but I had to stay over three hours, and I was supported by the Spirit to speak almost without a break for the whole of the time. Mr. Francis was moved to the quick. We had a meeting there and then. I went to prayer, then Francis, who was under the strongest feelings of brokenness".[8]

The minister's permission being received, the prayer meeting at Moriah that first Monday night was followed by a youth meeting. This consisted of a congregation of seventeen, one of them a little girl. Roberts recounted his recent experiences and visions and called upon all present to make public confession of Christ. "On Monday night I explained to them the purpose of my mission, and told them what the Spirit had wrought and was working at New Quay and Newcastle Emlyn. And I urged them to prepare for the baptism of the Holy Spirit."[9] The meeting was hard, the people unresponsive. He resorted to prayer three times during his long, protracted appeal. It was no easy task to overcome the prejudice of familiarity and the protocol of tradition. The people were naturally reserved, and were reticent about making public a conviction of soul in spiritual things until they had genuine experience of it. Eventually, however, all seventeen submitted.[10] The revival had been struggling for its very life, and without this victory at its inception all would have been lost. The remainder of that first crucial week, however hard it would prove to be, was gloriously assured by the experience at its first night of the omnipotence of God.

It was ten o'clock before they made their way home that night. For the revivalist it was a domestic triumph. He was returning home with the precious firstfruits of the revival from among his own family, his brother and three sisters having made open confession that very first night. Dan was overwhelmed with joy at the change in his own life and wrote later in the week to Sidney Evans, "I feel more joyful this week than ever before . . . Monday and Tuesday nights I felt the Spirit especially near. At times I want to weep, and the tears fill my eyes without any control whatsoever; at other times I want to sing. At home we now have family worship in which I take part, something I could never have done before."[11]   Before the end of the week Roberts was able to report to Sidney Evans : "There is a blessed change in our family. For the first time ever we have held family worship. This is also the work of the Spirit, and while I was away from home last Wednesday before the meeting they held a prayer meeting at home at which my father took part, the first time he ever did so in their hearing".[12]

If the night brought triumph, the morning thrust him back into severe trial. It came in the form of Satanic attack. "The devil troubled me sorely yesterday", he wrote on Wednesday, "asking me, what need was there for me to come from Newcastle Emlyn to Loughor to hold revival meetings, when there were enough ministers to be had? What right had I to waste my time? I now see that it is time for him to tremble, since his kingdom begins to shake."[13]   In another letter he adds : "It has been a glorious fight with the tempter, and, thank God, I am now victor. He tried to destroy my faith by saying . . . that God's Spirit was not with me, and that these remarkable influences were merely the fruit of my recounting the signs and visions I had seen."[14]

Six made open confession of Christ that Tuesday night at Pisgah. The congregation was more numerous, but the pattern remained the same. The meeting lasted three hours, several of those who had confessed Christ the previous night testifying to the joy of their new experience.[15]   Even at this early stage the characteristic emphases of his future meetings began to emerge : confession, prayer, and personal testimony. The importance of responding to the Spirit's impulse was impressed upon Roberts, and this principle became a prominent feature of the revival under his guidance. "The meeting last night was left entirely to the Spirit's direction. Reflecting on it I realized that the Spirit was teaching *obedience*."[16]

There seems to have been a more generous reception for Roberts at Libanus, Gorseinon, on the Wednesday night. He had agreed with the minister that after relating his experiences the revivalist should invite the youth to the Moriah meeting which was to follow. His audience at Libanus listened spellbound as he gave details of his visions and mentioned the Spirit's forecast of a widespread revival. Many followed him to Moriah, where they learned of the four-point plan for personal blessing revealed to him by the Spirit. The pattern of each meeting was becoming clearer. "This is the plan. Someone is asked to commence with a reading, another to announce a hymn, and yet another to pray. Then I say a few words."[17] These related to the four things which Roberts laid down as necessary to revival blessing.[18]

"1. If there is past sin or sins hitherto unconfessed, we cannot receive the Spirit. Therefore we must search and ask the Spirit to search. 2. If there is anything doubtful in our lives, it *must* be removed—anything we were uncertain about its rightness or wrongness. That thing *must* be removed. 3. An entire giving up of ourselves to the Spirit. We *must speak* and *do* all He requires of us. 4. Public confession of Christ."

The meeting was cold, difficult and unyielding, until someone from Moriah made a public confession of Christ, and this changed its tenor somewhat.[19].

Now his experience was reversed. Monday night's blessing had been followed by Tuesday morning's perplexity, whereas Wednesday night's gloom gave way on Thursday morning to a vision of hope. "A candle burned before me, behind it a rising sun in all its glory. What is the interpretation? In comparison to what is yet to come the revival at present is only as the light of a candle."[20] Reassured by this direct message from the Holy Spirit he made his way to the "seiat" at Moriah. The minister's arrival was delayed and Roberts was asked to lead the meeting. As he did so he was conscious of the sustained guidance of the Spirit. There was a distinct message to the children present, received directly from the Spirit, to be committed to memory and passed on to others : "the children were to learn this prayer, 'Send the Spirit to Moriah for Jesus Christ's sake' "[21]. It was so basic, he felt, that he commended it to others, as well as later developing the theme in his own meetings.

Roberts went on to explain his purpose, affirming his faith in God for the success of his mission. He reminded them of Christ's promises : "All power is given unto me in heaven and in earth . . . I am with you alway, even unto the end of the world" (Matt. 28 :18, 20); "Ask, and it shall be given you; seek and ye shall find" (Matt. 7 :7). These things were listened to with rapt attention by a large congregation. But at first there was an evident reluctance to make the public confession which Roberts required. It was only after much exhortation on his part that ten responded. Dissatisfied because Christ had not been glorified to the extent he expected or desired, the revivalist went on his knees in public prayer. "We are unwilling to leave this meeting until twenty have confessed Christ. O Lord, grant now another ten to those who have already done so !" During the time of deathly silence which followed, broken only by prayers and hymn singing, exactly ten more eventually submitted to the Spirit's promptings.[22]. When the meeting closed at 11 p.m., the prejudice of most had been removed, and the prospects of yet mightier blessings had become brighter. In many ways, that night's public trial of faith had been pivotal. Subsequent meetings were to grow in the intensity of the divine influences as well as in the numbers which attended them.

Understandably, perhaps, Roberts was deeply impressed and influenced by the direct nature of the Spirit's communication with him during those days. Not only had he been encouraged by visions, but also his faith had been strengthened by the message revealed for the children, and the knowledge given of the number of converts he should expect at the Thursday meeting. He was convinced that a visible representation of his visions on a printed postcard, after the fashion of the day, would give their messages the wider publicity which they deserved. On Friday morning therefore he wrote to the editor of the *Sunday Companion* with this in mind, asking for a quotation and adding, "We are on the eve of a great and grand revival, the greatest the world has ever seen. Do not think that the writer is a madman".[23] Its recipient was clearly "puzzled", but in his reply gave details of an electrotype agency. Recalling Roberts' letter over a year later the editor mentioned some of its other contents :

"He went on to say that the Holy Spirit had been working very much of late in the village in which he lived. That he and several others had been holding meetings, praying for the Holy Spirit to come down, and how they had wrestled with God until 2 or 3 o'clock in the morning. He went on to predict that a revival was coming to Wales, which would be the biggest that had been seen."[24]

Yet another vision came to him during the Friday evening meeting. This may have been nothing more than a pictorial representation in his imagination of the white and red horses of Revelation 6 :2, 4, scriptural references which he himself used when writing of it.[25]   Once again it had a confirmatory effect on his conviction regarding the certainty of the revival's success.   The Son of God was going forth to conquer with irresistible power.

The revivalist's activities were now beginning to attract public attention.   Consequently, by Friday's meeting the congregation was larger than ever, consisting of old as well as young, Baptists and Congregationalists as well as Calvinistic Methodists.   The following day he wrote :

"The leading characteristic of this work is that men are awakened to learn and obey.   The religious have had an entirely new and blessed experience.   They never dreamt before of the joy there is in open confession of Christ.   I arranged these meetings for young people, but old people flock along too . . .   Last night we commenced at 7; finished at 10 —those who had confessed Christ to remain.   Then the Spirit came near to us.   When I had prayed many of the people left for home, but some twenty stayed on, and we had a testimony meeting, praising the blessed Spirit for his wonderful work.   The meeting finished, or rather closed, at 11.30, and we could have gone on all night . . .   I believe there is to be a blessed revival in the near future."[26]

Already his experience had taught him to raise his expectancy from the level of a successful mission to that of a nation-wide revival.

Naturally, that raised the issue of his return to Newcastle Emlyn.   From the same letter it is evident that the very experiences, which had brought such joy to himself and blessing to others, now placed him on the horns of a dilemma. On the one hand, Thomas Francis' invitation to continue the meetings at Gorseinon was more compelling than ever, on the other he still felt some compunction about his studies.   A note

of indecision permeates the letter he wrote on the Saturday
morning :

"I intend returning to Newcastle Emlyn next Tuesday, if I
do not comply with Mr. Francis' request. He wishes me to
remain in his church for a week. I have not yet had God's
reply; I must obey His call. I want to pursue my studies and
prepare for the College, but I also want to work for my Friend
and Redeemer. This fire burns within me, and I am willing to
do His bidding."[27]

Another letter that same day seeks to resolve the difficulty.
It was sent to Sidney Evans and asked whether he would be
willing to accede to Francis' request.[28] This was more than a
diplomatic measure, for Evans' interest in working in Gorseinon was already known to Roberts.[29]

"Filled with the Spirit"

The crowded meeting that same night lasted over five
hours. Evan Roberts spoke on Ephesians 5 : 18, "Be not drunk
with wine, wherein is excess; but be filled with the Spirit".
He warned of the evils of drunkenness and, after a time of
prayer, proceeded to give a full and remarkable exposition of
the latter part of the verse. Writing to Florrie Evans about it,
he said :

"The Spirit was with us throughout last week; and last
night three women and one man were baptized with the Holy
Spirit. O! it was a fearful meeting. Everyone present
uttered this prayer—'Send the Spirit now, for Jesus Christ's
sake!' It was a chain prayer and everyone was to take part.
O! the effect was wonderful, and as the prayer went around,
one of the young men was filled with the Spirit . . we repeated the prayer a second time with this addition 'more

powerfully'—'Send the Spirit now more powerfully, for Jesus Christ's sake . . .' Now do not say 'Perhaps the Spirit will come', or 'we hope the Spirit will come', but 'We believe *He will come*'."[80]

The same procedure was adopted at the Sunday night meeting. It was characterized by some remarkable incidents. While Roberts went around the people urging them to confess Christ, one young lad stuttered as he pleaded with the congregation, "Pray for me", and instantly the whole congregation was overwhelmed with tears.

When midnight came Roberts called upon the people to concentrate on praying for the Holy Spirit, firmly believing that God would answer. Each one was to pray the same words without addition or elaboration, "Send the Holy Spirit *now,* for Jesus Christ's sake". Let the revivalist himself describe the scene which followed :

"I led in the prayer, then from seat to seat . . . I felt the place being filled, and before the prayer had gone half-way through the church, I heard some brother weeping—sobbing —and saying, 'O dear, dear !' 'Well, well !' 'O dear, dear !' The prayer went on, the influence intensifying, the place being filled more and more. Then I went to see the young man . . . 'What's the matter?' I asked. 'O', he replied, 'I've had something strange'. He went on to say that he felt his heart was too large for his bosom. I told him, 'You have received the Holy Spirit'. 'I do hope so', he said. Then the prayer had completed its *round,* but not its message. 'Shall we ask for still more?' 'No,' cried the young man. He had received as much as he could hold. But others had not received enough. So I said that one brother could hold no more, but that we would go on asking for more, and he could ask God to withhold if need be. God can give and withhold."[81]

The second round of prayer was to include the words "more powerfully", and as the meeting proceeded two women were filled with the Holy Spirit, and were unable to refrain from shouting loudly.

The sixty or so who had remained for this meeting had now gathered around the revivalist, well nigh overcome with awe, while he smiled reassuringly. Order gave place to confusion. Some were shouting, "No more, Lord Jesus, or I die!" Others cried for mercy. The noise of weeping, singing and praising, together with the sight of many who had fainted or lay prostrate on the ground in an agony of conviction was as unbelievable as it was unprecedented.[32] Eventually, with the singing of a well-known hymn, the final meeting of the first week came to an end and the revivalist made his way home. When he finally got to bed it was 3.15 a.m.

Similar scenes were witnessed on Monday night. News of the previous night's remarkable scenes was the talk of the locality throughout the day, and many gathered for the prayer meeting with the keenest anticipation. Evan Roberts spoke on the last chapter of Malachi, referring especially to the rising of the Sun of righteousness with healing in His wings. The pattern of the previous two nights was repeated with similar effects. The meeting ended at 3 a.m. In the midst of such spiritual activity he hardly found time to reflect on his dilemma, and when that night he was approached by representatives of the Congregational church, Bryn-teg, to take their meeting on Wednesday night he accepted without hesitation.[33]

By contrast Tuesday night's meeting was hard, protracted, and unresponsive. "Praying hard until four in the morning without any visible effect", was Roberts' summary of it. Nevertheless, some divine influences were felt toward the end of the meeting when only the younger element remained. In addition, he felt that the Spirit was teaching them to be concerned about the salvation of others and not merely their own.[34] The revivalist's mother had left wearily before the end, complaining that the men were asleep and would be unable to work; but she found herself in bitter conviction the next morning for her censorious spirit, and feared she was dying.[35] The blessing, however, was no longer confined to the revivalist's meetings. Thomas Francis spoke of the outburst of spiritual energy which had been felt in Gorseinon that very night. "In the prayer meeting there was grave silence, with each child present in communion with God, asking Him to send the Holy Spirit for Jesus Christ's sake. God answered their prayer and He descended on sons and daughters of all ages alike. We had never seen such weeping and singing and praying before."[36]

The Life of Faith, which appeared the next day (9th November) carried a contribution from Mrs. Penn-Lewis "telling of the 'cloud as a man's hand' which had risen over Wales". Her report was based on a letter she had received from Seth Joshua in October. Three weeks later she wrote to the same weekly paper, "We have prayed for revival. Let us give thanks! The 'cloud as a man's hand' . . . is now increasing. God is sweeping the southern hills and valleys of Wales with an old-time revival".[37]

That evening's meeting was held at Bryn-teg as arranged, and displayed much the same fervour as the Gorseinon meeting on Tuesday night. Roberts was overjoyed in spirit with a conviction that the meeting would be abundantly blessed. It continued for some eight hours with scenes of wild jubilation. One elder from Moriah came forward to embrace Roberts; his wife followed with a similar gesture, and when he sought opportunity to give public expression to his gratitude he was prevented from doing so by an overwhelming outburst of praise. Utterly unable to restrain himself the man clapped his hands, praised God, and laughed with sheer joy, while many of the congregation were on their feet or standing on the pews. Roberts felt constrained by the Spirit to make a missionary collection during this meeting, but the money could not be counted because of the powerful impressions which overcame the congregation.[38]

On Thursday Roberts found time to write some letters. He wrote with haste in a feverish excitement and the letters convey the sense of joyful elation which must have possessed his spirit to an unusual degree. They are filled with expressions of thankfulness after the previous night's triumphant scenes. "The Spirit descended in mighty power in Bryn-teg, Gorseinon, on Wednesday night. What a blessed sight! The women were shouting, singing, praying . . . Some fifteen or so were baptized with the Holy Spirit, I am not sure of the number. It is enough to know that God filled the place. Keep on praying fervently. This kingdom is bound to succeed in spite of what anyone says or does."[39] Writing to Elsie Phillips in London he recounts his experience thus :

"I came home to work under the guidance of the Holy Spirit, among our young people, but now I have to work under the guidance of the Holy Spirit among every denomination. The place of worship is full to the very doors and vestibule. The Spirit directed me to say that *three* things show that God is with us. 1. Enormous congregations. 2. Unity between the different denominations. 3. The baptism of the Holy Spirit. People came to see and hear 'the young lunatic'. Praise God 'the young lunatic' has been instrumental under the Spirit's direction in casting down many of sin's strongholds. Glory be to God! No! I am not mad, but full of the Spirit."[40]

If some derided him, others remembered similar pheno-

mena in the 1859 revival, and thereby urged him to continue
his revival ministry undaunted.

Even more astonishing were the scenes witnessed on
Thursday night. Many had come in their working clothes,
and at least one had brought the following day's packed lunch
with him! Some had travelled far to be present, an evidence
of widespread interest evoked independently of an elaborate
publicity campaign. In the midst of "this divine fire", as
Roberts referred to it, "the whole place has been stirred, and
my heart has been set ablaze by the Holy Spirit . . . The
people hold prayer meetings in their homes, family worship is
set up, and fellowship meetings are held in the steel works!"[41]

"Having favour with all the people"

This was the first meeting attended by a journalist from the
national daily, *The Western Mail*. Describing his impressions
of this meeting he says :

"I felt that this was no ordinary gathering. Instead of the
set order of proceedings to which we are accustomed at the
orthodox religious service, everything here was left to the
spontaneous impulse of the moment. The preacher, too, did
not remain in his usual seat. For the most part he walked up
and down the aisles, open Bible in hand, exhorting one, encouraging another, and kneeling with a third to implore a
blessing from the Throne of Grace. A young woman rose to
give out a hymn, which was sung with deep earnestness.
While it was being sung several people dropped down in their
seats as if they had been struck, and commenced crying for
pardon. Then from another part of the chapel could be
heard the resonant voice of a young man reading a portion of
scripture . . . Finally, Mr. Roberts announced the holding of
future meetings, and at 4.25 o'clock the gathering dispersed.

But even at this hour the people did not make their way home. When I left to walk back to Llanelly I left dozens of them about the road still discussing what is now the chief subject in their lives."[42]

Even though Roberts did not get home until 5 a.m., he was thankful that "Christ through His Spirit draws men to Himself", and that "girls of twelve and thirteen years of age receive the Spirit". [43]

Friday night's meeting was characterized by the intensity of conviction felt in it. Scores found themselves on their knees, unable to utter a syllable, and quite overcome with a sense of guilt. Some of these fell in a heap and others cried out pitifully and loudly in their desire for mercy. Meanwhile Evan Roberts was in spiritual agony, the perspiration pouring from his brow, as he prayed that God would glorify His Son and save sinners. So the meeting continued as a mighty spiritual upheaval until the dawn of a new day.[44] People lost all sense of time, and forgot their need for food, and were seemingly kept from physical exhaustion at their daily work. In the thick of the battle Roberts himself at any rate, was "in excellent health".[45]

Inevitably the *Western Mail* report of the Thurday night's meeting, which appeared on Saturday morning, gave the revival extensive publicity. It carried a more detailed description of the meetings than the first notice of the previous Thursday. That had been a fairly brief paragraph referring to "a remarkable religious revival" at Loughor and its effects on the life of the community : "Shopkeepers are closing earlier in order to get a place in the chapel, and tin and steel workers throng the place in their working clothes. The only theme of conversation among all classes and sects is 'Evan Roberts'. Even the taprooms of the public-houses are given over to dis-

cussion on the origin of the powers possessed by him".[46] The
result of such wide coverage was a great influx of people to
Loughor on the Saturday for the evening meeting.

Throughout the day there was intense spiritual activity.
Two young women held an open-air meeting in Gorseinon
which attracted a large crowd. Some went to a gipsy encamp-
ment at nearby Kingsbridge Common to hold a meeting,
resulting in the conversion of not a few from their midst. In
many homes in the area there were prayer meetings for most
of the day; eternal issues were discussed freely and un-
ashamedly, and, above all a sense of the presence and holiness
of God pervaded every area of human experience, at home, at
work, in shops and public houses. Eternity seemed inescap-
ably near and real.

Sidney Evans had returned home to Gorseinon that same
day, and was able to help Roberts at the evening meeting. He
related his experiences in Cardiganshire; and the meetings
(which were held in both new and old buildings at Moriah)
followed their customary course, ending at the usual early
hour of 5 a.m.[47] At the end of the second week it was
evident that the plans of the revivalist had been superseded by
the initiative of the Spirit, and the hopes of Evan Roberts had
been overshadowed by the power of God.

The return of Sidney Evans was not altogether a surprise.
Writing on Wednesday the 9th November he had anticipated
travelling on the Monday, but by Friday he felt constrained to
come home for the week-end.[48] This was entirely providential,
as Roberts' dilemma had been resolved in a totally unexpected
but decisive manner. Although he had received invitations
both to Ammanford and to Libanus, Pontardulais (each place
quite near his home) on the Thursday, he felt no freedom at
the time to accept them.[49] His reply to the latter invitation
gave as his reason the great burden of work at Loughor. It

continued : "Arrange prayer meetings . . . and pray especially for a powerful outpouring of the Holy Spirit. In addition,
let the children learn and pray the following prayer—'Send
the Holy Spirit to Libanus, for Jesus Christ's sake'."[50] Ammanford was a little distance further away from Loughor, and
their interest in revival generally and in Roberts particularly
had been aroused by a visit from Joseph Jenkins over the first
week-end of November.[51]

By the Thursday of the second week he had crossed his
Rubicon : he would not be returning to the school. Consequently when he wrote that morning to Sidney Evans he asked
for his luggage and intimated his decision regarding the
future : "I do not intend returning to school this term. Nor
have I time to do any school work while at home . . . Perhaps we shall have to go through the whole of Wales. If so,
thank heaven ! What a blessed time ! I am perfectly content
and blissfully happy with enough work from morning till
night."[52] The plans for his immediate future were crystallized
by a letter he received on Saturday, 12th November. It was
addressed to the minister of Moriah and read :

"I understand that there is a young preacher, Evan Roberts
by name, starting out in your midst, and according to a
report in yesterday's *Western Mail*, creating quite a stir. I
am pleased to hear this, and may the influence spread throughout the land. We in Bryn Seion, Aberdare, have been disappointed in our pulpit arrangements for next Sunday, 13th
November. Could you possibly get him to supply for us?"

Evan Roberts replied affirmatively the same day by telegram.[53]
It seemed to the revivalist that God was sending him from his
Jerusalem, and that the entire Principality was to be his
parish. There could be no doubt about one thing : his vision
was large enough to take it all in.

There was but little time to prepare for the train journey to Aberdare on Sunday morning. As he travelled he must have been apprehensive of the outcome. The newspaper reports had created a sense of expectancy in many people. Their response was to pray for a widespread visitation of God's Spirit in the land. Already the blessing was by no means confined to Loughor. There were simultaneous stirrings in other parts of Evan Roberts' extensive parish. The Spirit's sovereign operations were not limited to one place or to one man.

CHAPTER 7

SCATTERED BLESSINGS

TRUE revival is never limited by human personalities. The withdrawal of the leading figure from its scene need not diminish the heavenly influences, nor does it follow of necessity that the appearance of recognized instruments advances its progress. The matter is taken entirely out of human hands and rests with the divine prerogative. Independently of Evan Roberts the 1904 Revival continued unabated at Newcastle Emlyn and Loughor. In widely separated areas, where his name had yet to achieve fame, and at times prior to those when the fire fell on the as yet young "revival centres", there were undeniable evidences of unusual divine activity.

The Cardiganshire scene in those early days of November 1904 was still one of great spiritual excitement. Newcastle Emlyn itself had been the place of Sidney Evans' Pentecost experience, and, in answer to his prayers and those of Roberts, that of at least six others before the end of October.[1] On Roberts' departure for Loughor, Evans knew he would return to Gorseinon in due course, and that God would make known the appointed time.

Meanwhile he attended various meetings, some of which lasted over six hours, including convention and presbytery meetings, and an open-air meeting at Cardigan fair. At times his spirit would soar in the glow of success, at other times he felt the stinging blow of an onslaught from the devil.[2] Throughout this period, however, he was perplexed over the timing of his return to Gorseinon. On the 4th of November he wrote to Roberts, "My feelings are all mixed. I just do not know what to do. It is lonely here on my own, but I am perfectly willing to suffer this, as long as the Lord is with you at Loughor". Five days later there was only a glimmer of light : "I intend coming home on Monday, and find no rest in the idea . . . It is extremely difficult, and I am in great disturbance of mind. I have slept but little since Saturday".[3] By Friday the problem had been solved : "I shall come home tomorrow, but I'm not sure whether Florrie and Maud will be coming as well". On waking up the following morning his decision was confirmed, "I had orders to go home immediately".[4]

If their vision of itinerating throughout Wales as a team was not realized, Sidney Evans found consolation in visiting various churches in southern Cardiganshire with those from New Quay and Newcastle Emlyn who had been set ablaze by the Spirit's touch. They reciprocated prayer requests with Roberts, who, in turn, advised them as to procedure in an excited, terse manner :

"Establish revival meetings there. Call all the denominations together. Explain the 'four conditions'; and at the end of the meeting let all who have confessed Christ remain behind, and initiate the round of ejaculatory prayer. Take care that each one prays :

1. Send the Spirit *now,* for Jesus Christ's sake.

2. Send the Spirit *powerfully* now, for Jesus Christ's sake.

3. Send the Spirit *more powerfully* now, for Jesus Christ's sake.

4. Send the Spirit *still more powerfully* now, for Jesus Christ's sake.

Pray No. 1 over and over together, or individually as you are moved by the Holy Spirit; pray silently, too. Then No. 2 in the same way. No. 3 again. Finally No. 4. This is the Spirit's simple instrument."[5]

It is not clear from Evans' letters whether this scheme was used, but there is ample evidence that the effects were much the same. The reports he received from Loughor so far exceeded his expectations that he wrote with elation, "I rejoice that our prayers are answered so fully, and so soon . . . But nothing is too much to expect for *His Name's sake*. For myself, I expect the whole of Wales to be on fire with His praise . . . I believe all the devils of Gehenna have had their marching orders, and their kingdom will be crushed to the ground".[6]

Their labours at Loughor overlapped for only one night, that of Saturday, November 12th. While Evans recounted in the old building his experiences at Cardigan fair the previous day, Roberts supervised the scene of unparalleled excitement in the new. The meetings continued until 5 on Sunday morning. With Roberts' departure for Aberdare the focus of attention in the area switched to Evans' work at his home church of Libanus, Gorseinon. Commencing on the Sunday the revival meetings continued throughout the week, Florrie Evans and Maud Davies joining Evans on the Tuesday. Their contribution in prayer and song interspersed the testimonies, exhortations, prayers and songs of others.

According to Thomas Francis the meetings were entirely under the control of the Holy Spirit. Prayers were offered spontaneously for relatives and friends, the overwhelming desire being to spread the blessing to others.

"One young man sought his cousin. Having found him in the gallery he stood beside him, laid his hand on his shoulder, and prayed, 'Here he is, Lord; you know about him. He has drunk gallons of beer, but give him the water of life. That is so much better than beer . . .' In another meeting, he addressed the throne of grace . . . 'Christ's crumbs are better than the world's loaves' ".[7]

The crowds increased in size as the week went on, and visitors from places as far away as Bristol were present at the Friday meeting. Evans left on Saturday for one of the Glamorgan mining valleys, but the blessing continued at Gorseinon.[8]

Meanwhile in Cardiganshire the other students at the preparatory school followed the meetings for some time, but eventually gravitated back to their studies.[9] Joseph Jenkins' fourth convention was held at Tregaron, a market town some distance away from New Quay. The speakers were W. W. Lewis, W. S. Jones, and Mrs. Saunders. It was Jenkins' intention that the convention should fulfil a teaching ministry, and to some extent it did so. Contrary to his desire, however, "the ordinary people had lost patience. They had experienced the heavenly fire and were unwilling to listen or to be taught. They coveted 'freedom' and had an 'open meeting' with much blessing in it".[10]

Carmarthen

The same personnel brought blessing to the neighbouring county town of Carmarthen. The story goes back to the beginning of 1904, when the Free Church Council held a fortnight's mission under the leadership of Reader Harris. This was followed by another mission in March under W. R. Lane. Subsequently, prayer meetings for young people were held in Water Street chapel, and by June these had been signally blessed. They were followed by interdenominational open-air meetings during the summer months, through which many were converted. The period of quickened spiritual activity entered another phase in November with the visit of R. B. Jones—fresh from revival scenes in Rhos (North Wales)

—and Mrs. Penn-Lewis to a convention for the deepening of the spiritual life of the churches.

The climax of the year's spiritual harvest was reached during a conference arranged by the Calvinistic Methodists of the district shortly afterwards. It was at these meetings that Joseph Jenkins, J. M. Saunders and his wife ministered with powerful effects. The flood gates of blessing were opened, and on the last day of the conference "hardly a quarter of an hour passed without a number of people, young and old, men and women, in one part or another of Water Street chapel praying themselves or others from the bondage of sin to the liberty of the gospel". Other churches in the presbytery followed the same pattern with beneficial effects. Representatives from the different districts were called together for prayer and Bible study, and returned to their churches spiritually renewed and eager to spread the blessing. W. W. Lewis of Carmarthen was widely used in this ministry.[11]

Ammanford

Another of the Carmarthenshire towns, Ammanford, was in the midst of revival manifestations by the end of November. News of the New Quay meetings had been brought to the town by visitors and had created a longing for similar tokens of God's power. The church fellowship meeting at Bethany, the Calvinistic Methodist cause, turned to a consideration of past revivals, but by November the sense of expectancy and desire had waned considerably. The Sunday before Joseph Jenkins' engagement at the church, the minister, W. Nantlais Williams, preached on Acts 2 : 38-39, 'Then Peter said unto them, Repent, and be baptized every one of you in the name of Jesus Christ for the remission of sins, and ye shall receive the gift of the Holy Ghost. For the promise is unto you, and to your children, and to all that are afar off, even as many as the Lord our God shall call'. Following the sermon there was a proposal that prayer meetings should be held each night during the week. This was implemented, the attendances being higher than usual.

Preaching on Luke 19 : 10, 'For the Son of Man is come to seek and to save that which was lost', Jenkins exhorted the people in a colloquial manner, "Wrth ei draed cymerwch eich codwm yn deidi yn awr" (take your being made to fall humbly at his feet with good grace now). The sentence gripped the hearts of many and was to be used during the ensuing week. A heavenly nearness to God was felt by all present, and although there was no public outcry, the weeping was general throughout the congregation. At the afternoon meeting Jenkins spoke of the revival in New Quay, and as the meeting progressed the effect became so compelling that the congregation could not refrain from singing a Welsh hymn of gospel invitation to which the speaker had inadvertently referred.

It was not only the youth who responded to Jenkins' request that they should stay behind after the evening meeting. When he had set Christ's demands before them some gave a word of testimony, others prayed, but the most powerful influences were felt when a young woman read the verse of a hymn, 'Anweledig 'r wy'n dy garu, Rhyfedd ydyw nerth dy ras' (an expression of love to Christ for the power of grace). There were prayer meetings each night the following week. Jenkins had to leave on Tuesday morning, and that evening's prayer meeting was beset with difficulty for two hours.

"At last an unexpected dawn came. A young student who had been at one of Evan Roberts' meetings in Loughor got up, overwhelmed almost by strong emotions, saying, 'Someone here is making light of the Holy Spirit'. At this he broke down and tried to pray, but failed. Someone else got up to pray, and then yet another . . . Many young people openly confessed their sins, and in tears prayed for help and light."

The meetings became more and more powerful and prolonged as the week drew to its close. Children cried for salvation, and an older generation rejoiced. Friday's meeting continued until 2.30 a.m., and was spoken of as 'another Pentecost', some crying for mercy, others overpowered with joy.[12]

A week later Seth Joshua arrived in Ammanford for a mission. This had been arranged in consultation with Nantlais Williams and John Pugh some weeks previously, and was to have been a Forward Movement venture. The day before he travelled to Ammanford, Joshua was able to write in his diary, "Nov. 18 . . . I have wrestled for personal baptism of the Spirit and for a national revival. It has come and I rejoice".[13] He duly arrived the next day, just in time for his first meeting, quite unprepared for the scene which met his eyes. "At 7.30 I went to meet the workers in the chapel. To my surprise the chapel was filled with people. Seeing my opportunity I commenced at once, and at the close fully twenty confessed Christ. There is a wonderful fire burning here. The ground is very prepared, thank God."

The Sunday's services were typical of his experience throughout the mission :

"*Nov. 20.* This has been one of the most remarkable days of my life. Even in the morning a number were led to embrace the Saviour. In the afternoon the blessing fell upon scores of young people. The crush was very great to get into the chapel. At 7 o'clock a surging mass filled the Christian Temple, with crowds unable to gain entrance. The Holy

Spirit was indeed among the people. Numbers confessed Jesus, but it is impossible to count."

A snow storm on the Tuesday evening hindered many from attending, but Joshua could still record of the meeting, "a splendid audience and divine life sprang up . . . The doctrine of assurance is getting a deeper hold upon the people and many are being established". In spite of the snow the people spilled out on to the streets after the meetings and continued singing hymns until past midnight.

The spontaneity and intensity of the religious fervour at that time did not detract from its reality or permanence. Bookshops complained of the inadequacy of their supply of Bibles. The coal mines were transformed by the sound of praise in the place of blasphemous oaths. The public houses were empty of rowdy customers and the homes were full of joy and singing.[14] During the Christmas vacation a Cardiff student was deeply impressed by the open-air witness of a converted man, formerly notorious for his reckless and ungodly living :

"At the square that night I joined a crowd listening to someone speak from a platform. When I saw who it was I could hardly believe my eyes, for I knew him well, and everyone else knew him to be one of the profanest characters in the area. There he was . . . with sentences and verses of Scripture pouring forth from his lips. I did not know the story of his conversion but I knew of the fluency and blasphemy of his oaths previously. That sudden view of him, so fervently commending the salvation which is in Christ to the surrounding crowd, shook me".[15]

To these new converts the timing of Joshua's ministry was nothing short of providential, and its quality was directly appropriate. As Nantlais Williams commented later, "He knew of every step in the spiritual life, from the public house, or as Joshua himself put it, 'from the sawdust of the taproom', to the heavenly places in Christ Jesus".[16]

Ammanford is noteworthy because it was later to become the venue of an annual convention for the deepening of the spiritual life. It was initiated in 1917 by Nantlais Williams, who traced his conversion experience to the revival. Until that time his ambition had been to succeed as a popular preacher and poet. Although he had preached about the Holy Spirit on the Sunday before Jenkins' visit, he knew but little of the Spirit's gracious influences in his experience. In the week which followed he spent a whole night "to knock and plead at the door of mercy" without any release. At the Saturday night meeting, however, as he joined almost involuntarily in the hymn-singing he felt a heavenly joy in his soul.

"Having sat down on returning home I realized, quietly and without any great commotion, that it is by *believing* we receive salvation; not through effort and anguish in prayer all night on my part, but through the wrestling of Another for me in the Garden, and on the cross; yes, by relying on him and his bloody sweat and dying agony. O! what deliverance! What peace! I believed, because the way of life had been unmistakably revealed to me. Well, well. So simple, so near, so plain, so free! The way of salvation is so endearing in its conditions!"[17]

He was soon to find that it was no less demanding than endearing, as the joy of deliverance gave way to the joy of service. The experience was not without a resulting personal sacrifice. 'The young bard of Ammanford' was publicly commended and encouraged shortly afterwards by Cynddylan

Jones for taking a bold stand in preaching : "Go on, preach
forgiveness on the part of God and assurance of forgiveness
on the part of men, for that is the law and the prophets, that
is the Bible and the Creed, that is the gospel and the Confession of Faith".[18]

With the ripening of his spiritual understanding he felt
constrained to deny himself the lawful inclination to be
absorbed with eisteddfod pursuits, on the grounds of its in-
expediency to the service of Christ. He also gave himself
entirely to his own church, a step for which he was mis-
understood. In the public press he was reported to have
joined the Plymouth Brethren, and many doors of service
were closed to him.[19] In spite of misrepresentation and
slander his contribution to Calvinistic Methodism was invaluable, as a leader of evangelical witness, editor of his denomination's monthly periodical *Trysorfa'r Plant* (Children's Trea-
sury), and the author of many Welsh hymns.

Tonypandy in the Rhondda

Exceptionally powerful stirrings of the Holy Spirit had
been experienced at Tonypandy in the Rhondda since the
beginning of 1904. Indeed, one report stated that for four
years Trinity, the English Calvinistic Methodist cause, had
seen visible fruit each week in the usual means of grace, so
that by October 1904, over 600 had already professed conversion.[20] Even before Evan Roberts' visit the place had
therefore witnessed the power of God at work in a great
variety of operations.

"Among these (conversions) were some of the worst characters in the district. Men and women of all ages took part in
the services. Some who were on their way to the theatre,
the billiard-room, and other places of amusement, when they

heard the singing in the chapel, felt constrained to retrace their steps and to enter the building, with the result that they made a confession, and expressed a desire to lead a different life."[21]

One correspondent, writing to a denominational weekly in February, 1904, spoke of the warm fervour of the churches and their zeal to save souls. "There are prayer meetings either in the church, or in derelict buildings, or on the streets every night here, and often in two or three places at once."[22]

London

Further away from Loughor, the Welsh community in London was stirred in the early days of the revival. Roberts' letters to Elsie Phillips supplied accounts of his work at Loughor, and she commenced prayer meetings at the Welsh Calvinistic Methodist church at Willesden Green. She was hopeful of a happy issue : "I believe God will set this little church ablaze one day. A good number of the young people have bent the knee to the Redeemer. One of the young men was formerly an atheist, and all I can say is, thank God he has realized his mistake, and now joins with our holy company to work for Jesus Christ".

About this time a visiting minister from Cardiganshire, Rhystyd Davies, supplemented her efforts by giving accounts of the revival in the New Quay area. The influence spread to other Calvinistic Methodist churches at Charing Cross Road, Hammersmith, Falmouth Road, and Lewisham. Elsie Phillips visited the latter church, witnessing scenes of praying and singing similar to those at Loughor. Newspaper reports of the Welsh revival gave added impetus to the prayer meetings set up in the various churches.[23]

The blessing was confined mainly to the Welsh churches,

but in January, 1905, there were reports that a church in South Bermondsey under W. K. Dunn had been richly blessed. The minister had visited the scenes of the revival in South Wales with much personal profit, and on his return had witnessed the spreading of the heavenly fire in and around his church. Of the 200 converts in this place over half had been drunkards.[24] Amongst the Welsh community at Stratford the revival meetings continued to make progress in May, 1905, having received fresh impetus by the visit of two lady evangelists from South Wales. The meetings were as fervent as those in the Welsh valleys, and some English visitors were coming under the revival influences.[25] A fortnight's mission to the London Welsh churches at about this time, conducted by six Welsh students, claimed 720 converts.

North Wales

In North Wales there were signs of the coming blessing at a fellowship meeting in Barmouth, Merionethshire, as early as January, 1902, while a little country church in Anglesey felt powerful spiritual influences from which there issued strong leadership in later years. Early in May of that year similar experiences were felt at the Towyn District meeting of the Wesleyans. The occasion was a theological day conference at which a paper was read on 'The Holy Spirit and His work'. In the discussion which followed everyone was under unusually solemn impressions. There was an outburst of song and praise, and one report spoke of a supernatural brilliance reflected in the faces of all who were present. The representatives returned from that meeting with renewed longing for revival, and the matter became a talking point throughout the district.[26] The spontaneous breaking forth of praise when the preacher announced his text was reported from one church several months later, in December.[27]

Bethesda

Further north, at Bethesda, the Free churches felt the need for a joint evangelistic effort because of the adverse spiritual and moral effects of a strike in the slate quarries. This was held from the 21st to the 24th of November, the missioner being Hugh Hughes, a Wesleyan minister. The spiritual influences were felt most powerfully in the prayer meetings. Each evening's meeting was preceded by an hour's prayer meeting, and followed by a young people's prayer meeting, which sometimes lasted for three hours. Some 500 women were attending an afternoon prayer meeting, and this was usually the scene of agonizing prayer and weeping, interspersed with fervent song and spontaneous testimony.

Hugh Hughes returned later for a further three nights, preaching the gospel with simplicity and power. The effects now reached the ungodly in the community and many were converted, while the young people were hardly able to close their prayer meeting at midnight. By the 3rd of December some twenty had professed conversion and the moral tone of the village had been radically transformed. One of the ministers jubilantly reported : "The policemen tell me that the public houses are nearly empty, the streets are quiet, and swearing is rarely heard. Things are easy for the policemen here now—I hope they have a glorious holiday, and the district is quite prepared to support them henceforth—for doing nothing!"[28] A newspaper report claimed : "The results have been most gratifying, especially in the healing of old quarrels and feuds which had been caused by the Penrhyn (quarry) strike".[29]

The divine work in their midst was further implemented by the preaching of visiting ministers during December, especially that of Joseph Jenkins. Accompanied by Maud Davies and Florrie Evans, he stayed with one of the local ministers, John T. Job, who spoke of the sleepless nights spent in talking, praying, and singing. "The revival was everything; talking about Christ's mighty works in Cardiganshire, especially among the Aberystwyth students; the young girls singing and weeping; sharing experiences of the Holy Spirit; each one of us praying all the while into the early hours of the morning."[30] His own experience was deeply enriched during this period : "I felt the Holy Spirit as a torrent of light shaking my entire nature . . . I have done nothing since that night except sing quietly to myself that verse 'O, anfeidrol rym y Cariad! Anorchfygol ydyw'r gras; Digyfnewid yw'r addewid . . .' (O! the immensity of Love's power; how irresistible the grace; how unchangeable the promise . . . !). I have found myself laughing for hours on end by myself in this house, and I feel I can pray by laughing these days!"[31]

The effects of Jenkins' preaching could only be compared to those on the day of Pentecost. His sermon was preceded by over an hour's prayer meeting, and his emphasis on the divine initiative in the work of sanctification (based on Philippians 2 : 13) was brought home to the congregation so powerfully that the meeting broke up in heavenly disorder. The verse of the Welsh hymn 'Y Gŵr a fu gynt o dan hoelion dros ddyn pechadurus fel fi' (The Man who suffered under the nails for a sinful man like me) was repeated several times. Many of the congregation, in the ecstasy of their spiritual deliverance, were unable to restrain themselves from dancing without either inhibition or irreverence. At the young people's prayer meeting which followed, the noise of prayer (some dozen or so praying simultaneously), weeping and shouting was at once deafening and harmonious.[32]

The children, too, experienced the blessings of the revival, meeting frequently for prayer, and even at school using the playtime for that purpose.[33] It was a full two months later that Evan Roberts paid a 'surprise visit' to the Bethesda singing festival.[34] By that time the entire area had experienced in abundant measure the varied effects of revival.

Among the converts perhaps the most widely known was William Hughes. Driven from home by unemployment, he had roamed far afield in search of work and found himself in the closing months of 1904 working as a miner in one of the Glamorgan pits. Brought under conviction while attending one of Dan Roberts' meetings, he experienced bitter remorse and intense spiritual conflict. There were times of mental torment at the remembrance of past sins when his whole physical frame would be overwhelmed with uncontrollable shivering. He longed to be alone with God, so that he could shout his confession and cry for mercy without restraint. At last the opportunity came when he was working underground on a lonely section of the coal face.

"He entered the familiar 'man-hole'—the miner's place of refuge from the coal trucks passing—and he felt as if the air were thick with his own curses of bygone days. Then with a cry and shout, as if his whole nature were being rent, he prayed for God's mercy and help. And as he cried, he felt as if a physical burden were being lifted from him, borne on slow, strong wings through the roof of the mine, and away for ever. The worst of the conflict was over in that one tremendous moment. Tears came, but their bitterness was gone; songs came, with or without words, but all-triumphant."[35]

Joyfully, he made his way home for Christmas. In the days which followed, the transformation in his life attracted many of his old companions in sin to seek spiritual counsel in his home, which became 'a surgery of wounded souls'. With commendable perseverance he gave himself to studying the Bible and doing the work of an evangelist in his native community. Several months later, in June, 1905, he took a prominent part at one of Evan Roberts' meetings in Anglesey, exclaiming in prayer, "I was one of the devil's chieftains, but tonight I am labouring in the vineyard".[36]

Reports of the revival in South Wales had been given at a presbytery meeting at Pwllheli on the 28th of November, but interest in religious exercises was already being shown in many parts of the county from Llanfairfechan to Llanberis.[37] By the 9th of December the *Caernarvon and Denbigh Herald* could report, "The religious revival appears to be rapidly spreading throughout North Wales. Meetings are held practically at every town, and great enthusiasm prevails". Generally speaking a common pattern was followed in most areas; on hearing of the revival, interdenominational prayer meetings were commenced, with or without preaching services, in which the young people took a prominent part. The effects were usually the same; church members were solemnized and became more fervent in their prayers, numbers were converted, swearing and drunkenness were virtually eliminated, and the overwhelming sense of God's presence made spiritual issues an easy and compelling topic of conversation. An indication of the extent of these influences is the fact that, in the granite quarries of Penmaen-mawr and Llanfairfechan the workmen were holding "prayer meetings of the most impressive character every dinner hour".[38]

The Nantlle Valley

The Nantlle valley to the south-west of Bethesda was also a slate-quarrying area. Before the end of 1904, and independently of Evan Roberts' ministry, it was to become one of the leading centres of the revival in North Wales, and one of its sons, Evan Lloyd Jones, was to be reckoned a northern counterpart of Roberts himself.[39]　He first came into prominence at a revival meeting in Tal-y-sarn at which Joseph Jenkins and the two girls from New Quay took part.　Having ascended into the pulpit Jones spoke of the previous night's experience at Nebo when in response to his appeal a large number of young people had unitedly and successfully prayed for the Holy Spirit's anointing.　The heavenly glory seemed to fill the place in a most wonderful and memorable way.[40]

The son of a local miner, he was at the time assisting as a teacher at the Nebo village school.　An irresistible spiritual authority was the most remarkable feature of his revival ministry.　Although only twenty years of age he controlled the meetings with the discernment and skill of an experienced campaigner.　One of the converts testified that his face shone with such brilliance that they became oblivious of all else in the meeting, and could in no way reject Christ in spite of the mighty efforts they made to leave the building.[41]

At first his activities seem to have been confined to the Nantlle district, but by February, 1905, he was being used in the towns along the North Wales coast as well as in the villages of the Lleyn peninsula.[42]　Others who ministered widely in this north-west corner of the Principality included Joseph Jenkins, D. M. Phillips, and H. Elvet Lewis.

One of the most astonishing incidents of the revival took place at Pwllheli in January, when a political meeting, convened for the member of Parliament and later Prime Minister, David Lloyd-George, metamorphosed naturally and irresistibly into a religious service.　When the two political speakers walked on to the platform they were hardly noticed.　Instead, after opening devotions by a minister of religion, the audience sang a Welsh hymn with unusual fervour, and a blind man led in prayer.　In extolling the effects of the revival, Lloyd-George compared it to a tornado sweeping over the country and

bringing in its train far-reaching national and social changes.[43]
On a previous occasion he had compared the revival to "a
mighty earthquake", and at a public gathering in Glasgow
had spoken of a town in his constituency where the total
takings in a public house one Saturday night had been 4½d![44]

Egryn

Further south in Merionethshire, on the main road between Harlech castle and Barmouth beach, lies another in-
significant village like Nebo, Egryn. Its fame in 1904 was
mainly due to the supernatural visions and evangelistic fervour
of an ordinary housewife, Mrs. Mary Jones. As a middle-
aged farmer's wife her revival activities were phenomenal, if
not unique; witness a contemporary assessment :

"The mission of this woman evangelist is unparalleled, just
as that of Evan Roberts. These are the two leading figures
in the field today in Wales. Both have emerged from the
ranks of the ordinary people, quite untutored. They were
both nurtured in villages on the seaboard and were the pro-
ducts of the 'seiat'. They had experienced the most exacting
spiritual discipline and had seen the most remarkable visions.
Having received a special message from the living God they
were both moved by the Holy Spirit at about the same time
to proclaim it, until a whole nation has been awakened and
set alight."[45]

Without previous preparation or instruction Mrs. Jones
was sent forth by God, as she believed, to be a prophetess of
the Most High, and she exercised that rare office as one born
out of due time.

The local Calvinistic Methodist cause had persevered with
its prayer meeting throughout the busy pastoral summer.
With news of revival stirrings in Cardiganshire increasing

interest was shown in it during October. Towards the end of a week of prayer Mrs. Jones publicly interceded at the throne of grace for the salvation of all, with evident anguish of soul. She was the first woman to do so. The congregation was instantly overcome with strong spiritual impressions.[46] This took place shortly before a presbytery meeting at which reports were given of the revival in the various churches, providing a stimulus to many others to seek similar blessings themselves.[47]

From that time Mrs. Jones took over the spiritual leadership of the church at Egryn, and her zeal for bringing others to Christ was proverbial. On the way to the church she would see lights in the sky in the form of a pillar of fire, a claim which was substantiated by several independent witnesses.[48] She interpreted these as specific guidance from God in such matters as, for instance, where she should visit, and how many converts would result from a particular meeting. Some seventy souls were added to the church at Egryn in that period. On one occasion the Holy Spirit's operations were so powerful that Mrs. Jones pleaded, "O Lord, stay your hand until I have put on immortality".[49]

Rhosllanerchrugog

The story of the revival at the mining district of Rhos (Rhosllanerchrugog) near Wrexham begins with Rosina Davies early in 1904. Her mission, held under Free Church auspices, was 'exceptionally successful' both on account of its numerical results and solemn tone.[50] Even stronger stirrings were felt in the Baptist church at nearby Ponciau in June. The annual preaching festival on Sunday and Monday, the 19th and 20th, was so uncommonly blessed that the congregation was compelled to continue with prayer meetings and further preaching services. Throughout the Sunday the influences had become more and more powerful, so that the entire district awaited Monday's services with a sense of expectancy. Both ministers, Thomas Shankland and J. R. Jones, preached in the evening, on Ephesians 3 : 21 and Isaiah 55 : 11-12 respectively. The power of the Holy Spirit felt at that time was compared to the effects of the 1859 revival by the older members.[51]

Similar scenes were witnessed at the Baptist church in Rhos itself when R. B. Jones commenced a ten-day mission there on the 8th of November. At first he directed his ministry to the church, preaching on Isaiah 6, reserving his appeal to the unconverted to the second week. The closing meeting was unprecedented in its length, lasting from 10 a.m. to 10 p.m., with the local ministers assisting in turn. After Jones' sermon on 1 Timothy 1 : 15 in the evening the congregation gave way to general jubilation, praise, prayer, and testimony.[52] In the words of one commentator, Rhos was "ablaze, and the converts number one hundred already".[53] The heavenly conflagration was maintained on an interdenominational basis during the subsequent months by the visits of preachers like W. W. Lewis, Hugh Hughes, H. Elvet Lewis, and General William Booth.[54]

The intensity of the revival at Rhos was sustained well into the following March. Early in that month (4th) the *Rhos Herald* published the numbers of the converts in each of the district's churches, the total being 2,267. According to one estimate the most remarkable meeting of the revival was not until the 20th of that month. This was an afternoon prayer meeting. Scores of people took part in prayer simultaneously, large numbers were completely overcome, and the entire congregation was in tears.[55]

Another remarkable day at Rhos was December 7th. The meeting held on that day "seemed to be prayer from first to last; the form varied—speech, song, supplication; but it was all prayer". The same reporter tells of the conversion of a notoriously godless character at the meeting, when the congregation was apprehensive of his motives :

"They saw the face, stained with perspiration and tears, and at the first glance, more terrifying than usual; but there was a gleam of new life upon it. 'None of you will ever know,' he began, in a voice part shout, part sob, 'what I have passed through tonight. I have wept a pool of tears where I have been sitting, and they were the gladdest tears I ever knew. The agony before that!—my head seemed to swell and swell, as if it would at last burst. But it grew easier when the tears came. You all know me; you know for whom I have fought; but I am changing sides tonight, to fight on the side of Jesus'."

His conversion proved genuine, and in time all thirteen of the reckless gang which he had led in sin were brought to Christ.[56]

The revival affected Rhos deeply. Prayer meetings were held in the coal mines, processions of converts were commonplace even among the children, family feuds and quarrels were resolved, and the cause of temperance especially was strengthened. As Christmas approached one converted drunkard resolved, "I shall spend this Christmas in a different way from all others. I used to think of nothing but getting drunk, but this year I shall drink pure wine from Calvary's cellar".[57]

Thus November, 1904, had brought great joy to the widely separated districts of Rhos and Loughor, to North as well as South Wales. Geographically distant, yet independently and simultaneously, the powerful convictions and jubilant conversions in both north and south alike were defined by means of the same biblical term : Pentecost. The staggering success of the gospel could not be attributed to the instrumentality of any one man, nor even to the combined efforts of all. This was not the wisdom of man, but the power of God. It did not belong to the categories of psychological techniques, publicity methods, and personality cults. On the contrary, there were evident signs of God's sovereign power : the sense of God's presence, the open acknowledgment of fundamental saving truths, and the lasting quality of transformed lives.

In all these things the faithful instinctively recognized the hand of God.

CHAPTER 8

INSPIRED ITINERARY

THROUGHOUT the winter of 1904-05 Evan Roberts and the revival attracted unprecedented publicity. The *Western Mail*, catering mainly for South Wales, was especially sympathetic, giving detailed and extensive coverage of the meetings. These articles were subsequently collected together and issued in the form of a pamphlet under the title *The Religious Revival in Wales*, a total of six appearing by May, 1905. The team of reporters followed Roberts' itinerary, although they were not strictly confined to it. As the revival progressed, so the news received wider attention, newspapers even in Catholic countries such as France, Italy and Portugal giving several columns and pictures to their reports.

An influx of visitors

One direct result of this was the increasingly cosmopolitan nature of the revival congregations. It became possible to claim for the Rhondda valley meetings that "persons from all directions appear in the congregation; from France, Russia, America, England, and Scotland, and all parts in Wales".[1] In February 1905 the remote village of Nant-y-moel in Glamorganshire was visited for the same purpose by "three ladies from Germany who did not understand even English, six French gentlemen, a lady sent from Paris by the church with which she is connected, two missionaries on a visit to this country from China, and dozens of Scottish, English, and North Wales clergymen, preachers, and laymen".[2] No less impressive was the list of visiting personalities, among them F. B. Meyer, G. Campbell Morgan, Gipsy Smith, Ferrier

Hulme (Bristol), Hugh Black (Edinburgh), F. S. Webster (All Souls', Langham Place, London), Dr. A. McCaig (Principal of Spurgeon's College), K. Behesmilan (Armenia), and Cadod de Chauney (France).

There were countless others who were unable to make the journey to the Principality. One of these was R. A. Torrey, confined to Liverpool by his mission activities. On reading of the revival he wrote the following letter to Roberts, dated 29th November, 1904 :

"I have heard with great joy of the way in which God has been using you as the instrument of his power in different places in Wales. I simply write you this letter to let you know of my interest in you, and to tell you that I am praying for you. I have been praying for a long time that God would raise up men of his own choosing in different parts of the world, and mightily anoint them with the Holy Spirit, and bring in a mighty revival of his work. It is so sadly needed in these times.

"I cannot tell you the joy that has come to my heart, as I have read of the mighty work of God in Wales. I am praying that God will keep you, simply trusting in him, and obedient to him, going not where men shall call you, but going where he shall lead you, and that he may keep you humble. It is easy for us to become exalted when God uses us as the instruments of his power. It is so easy to think that we are something ourselves, and when we get to thinking that, God will set us aside. May God keep you humble, and fill you more and more with his mighty power.

"I hope that some day I may have the privilege of meeting you."[3]

Many wrote requesting prayer for their respective countries; Ireland, Scotland, England, Norway, France, Spain,

Africa. Roberts for his part was convinced "that the Spirit which prevailed so largely in Wales today would spread not only to England, but throughout the world".[4] His prophecy was fulfilled, and places as far apart as India and Latin America later experienced powerful visitations.

Evan Roberts in Glamorgan

The immediate sphere of Roberts' ministry, however, was limited to his native county of Glamorgan. His acceptance or refusal of the pressing invitations he received was determined solely on the basis of the Spirit's constraint. Moreover, he felt no compunction in revising his itinerary whenever such a course was dictated by the Holy Spirit. On this account his proposed visit to Cardiff, for instance, was postponed indefinitely. The day before his agreed engagement in the city he was seen by J. Morgan Jones, a Cardiff minister, and the following conversation ensued:

"Mr. Jones asked the revivalist if he were coming to Cardiff on the morrow.

" 'No,' replied Evan Roberts, with considerable emphasis.

" 'Are you still too unwell to come?' questioned Mr. Jones.

" 'No, it isn't that,' returned Mr. Roberts. 'I am feeling quite well and strong.'

"Obvious surprise was depicted on Mr. Jones' face, and he again asked the revivalist why he was not coming to Cardiff.

" 'The Cardiff meetings have been on my mind for five days,' replied Mr. Roberts. 'I have prayed constantly for guidance, and the answer of the Spirit is "Thou art not to go".'

"Mr. Jones observed that there was a close connection between the body and the mind. Was Mr. Roberts sure that he did not mistake bodily weakness or reluctance for the answer of the Spirit?

" 'I am as certain that the Spirit has spoken to me,' returned the evangelist, still speaking in Welsh, 'as I am of my own existence.' "

Nevertheless, this subjectivism in his principles of guidance was not without its safeguards. It was consistently applied, even though its application might appear arbitrary and erratic to others.

If the limits of its authenticity were confined by the humanity of the instrument, they were also regulated by biblical categories of reference and a God-centred motivation :

"It is known that Mr. Roberts had a presentiment that his mission in Cardiff would not be divinely favoured; in fact, he clearly stated that a divine voice told him that he was not to go to Cardiff. In the course of a conversation with a local ministerial friend, Mr. Roberts declared that the voice said, 'If you go I shall not go with you', and on its being pointed out to him that his non-appearance would be a serious disappointment to many thousands in Cardiff, he said, 'I can't help it; I am not going with this voice ringing in my ears'. He was then asked, 'What about the crowds that will be expecting you?', and he replied, 'That is it; I want to be in the background'."[5]

The danger of the subjectivist element lay in its tendency to establish an autocratic disposition, especially in the face of opposition. This left the revivalist's rôle open to misunderstanding by others and misinterpretation by himself. On occasions the delicate balance between biblical considerations and personal inclination showed sufficient deviation to bring about the exaltation of human expediency at the expense of divine providence.

The distinctly cool reception which Roberts received at Trecynon on Sunday, November 13th, might have caused him concern, if not doubt, as to the validity of these principles. The crowds were absent, the fervour was low, the congregation hesitant. Undaunted, the revivalist and his team of five ladies from Gorseinon persevered, and their faith was rewarded. Scenes such as those witnessed at Loughor were repeated, bringing to the minds of some memories of the 1859 revival.

The outbursts of prayer and praise in the meetings were spontaneous and intense, while Roberts walked along the aisles, his face radiant with joy. In the days which followed there were "scores of conversions, including sceptics, backsliders, drunkards of the worst class, and self-righteous persons. One noted agnostic burned all his books, and went about to other places to offer Christ to sinners."[6]

From Trecynon the revivalist went to Pontycymmer in the Garw coal-mining valley. Spiritual excitement ran high as his coming was anticipated, partly on account of the widespread publicity he had received, and partly because he was coming on the invitation of the united religious bodies of the area. Already people were referring to him as "the John Wesley of Wales", and the crowds came from near and far, many out of no higher motive than curiosity. The most remarkable feature of the work at Pontycymmer was the prayer meeting when, according to one witness, "Mr. Roberts fell prostrate and remained on his face on the floor for some time. He seemed to be in agony".

The following morning at 5 o'clock he was at the pithead "waiting for the night shift to come up from below. When the men appeared he shook hands with them all, and invited those of the men who were not too tired to come to the prayer meeting. Most of them came. Stirring scenes were witnessed, strong men of rough exterior sobbing almost hysterically, and bearing testimony in quivering, broken accents."[7] The transformation in the lives of the miners gave new pathos to their singing and fresh originality to their prayers. It was one such workman who exclaimed in prayer, "We have seen Satan's worst many times, but have never seen Christ's best until now".[8]

Conversions amongst the coal-miners

During the months of November and December the revival was in its purest phase. Roberts' bearing and speaking seemed to be inspired, the deepest and most lasting work was done among the people, and excesses were most effectively restrained. The section of the community most affected by the heavenly fire was undoubtedly the coal-miners. Underground, the coal seams echoed their praises and the coal faces witnessed the conversion of many of the workers.

The revival was not without its social impact in the mines. Some colliery managers claimed that the revival had made their workers "better colliers", others spoke of "greater regularity in the attendance of the men at work". Even trade union disputes were affected by the revival, as the story of a man charged with "filling dirty coal" shows :

"He told the officials that he would 'make them sit up for it', because he would get the works committee to take it up with the Miners' Federation. Instead of going to the committee, he went to hear Evan Roberts, who talked about the Spirit in a man's heart making it impossible for him to do a mean action, and the result was he went back to the colliery office, and asked to be allowed to work on, that he did not intend bringing anything before the works committee, and that he would never again give cause of complaint about 'dirty coal' being filled into his trams. Needless to say, his offer was promptly accepted."[9]

At a time when disputes between management and the unions were becoming common, the beneficial effect of the revival on industrial relations can hardly be over-estimated, and has hitherto been unrecognized.

A typical underground scene is described by a contemporary writer in the *Western Mail* :

"The workmen on the night shift had gone down half an hour earlier than the usual time so as not to interfere with the operations of the pit. Seventy yards from the bottom of the shaft, in the stables, we came to the prayer meeting. One of the workmen was reading the 6th chapter of Matthew to about eighty comrades. He stood erect amongst the group, reading in a dim, fantastic light that danced with the swinging lamps and vanished softly into surrounding darkness. A number of lamps were attached to a heavy post closely wedged to support the roof, and around the impressive figure the colliers grouped themselves . . . Earnest men, all of them; faces that bore the scars of the underground toiler; downcast eyes that seemed to be 'the homes of silent prayer'; strong frames that quivered with a new emotion."

A hymn followed the reading, then an impromptu exhortation, occasionally supported by fervent "Amens", and succeeded by prayers until the time came for work to be commenced. "Not once, but many times, was God's blessing asked for the honest and proper execution of the work."[10]

Roberts was not always first on the scene of such revival manifestations. The movement was "sweeping like a wave" over most of the mining valleys of Glamorgan by the end of November. At Porth, for example, R. B. Jones had seen much blessing almost a week before Roberts' first visit. Prayer meetings held a fortnight before his coming to Ynys-y-bwl had been characterised by the remarkable earnestness of the young people.[11] Before he reached Tylorstown the churches had registered some 200 converts,[12] while at Morriston, Sidney Evans could report over 300 converts in a week by December 4th, and over four times that figure had been recorded by the end of the month when Roberts eventually arrived. The revivalist did not visit Maerdy in the Rhondda until December 11th, by which time "no less than 500 converts" had already been counted.[13]

The leading of the Spirit

"The most extraordinary thing about the meetings which I attended", said W. T. Stead, a London journalist who arrived in Maerdy on the same day, "was the extent to which they were absolutely without any human direction or leadership." His description continues : " 'We must obey the Spirit' is the watchword of Evan Roberts, and he is as obedient as the humblest of his followers. The meetings open—after any amount of preliminary singing, while the congregation is assembling—by the reading of a chapter or a psalm. Then it is go-as-you-please for two hours or more. And the amazing thing is that it does go and does not get entangled in what might seem to be inevitable confusion. Three-fourths of the meeting consists of singing. No one uses a hymn-book. No one gives out a hymn. The last person to control the meeting in any way is Mr. Evan Roberts. People pray and sing, give testimony; exhort as the Spirit moves them. As a study of the psychology of crowds, I have seen nothing like it. You feel that the thousand or fifteen hundred persons before you have become merged into one myriad-headed, but single-souled personality."[14]

This pattern was typical. It was not only in the matter of guidance as to his movements that the revivalist relied on the impulse of the Spirit. The character, conduct, and progress of each meeting was evidently determined by the same token.

For Evan Roberts the liberty of the Spirit was not only a God-given principle to be advocated and exercised, it was also a privilege to be jealously guarded. There were many in the revival meetings who manipulated this liberty into licence for their own advantage. It was all too easy for a misguided zeal to mistake the manifestation of the flesh for the gift of the Spirit. Towards the end of 1904, for instance, the *Western Mail* reporter complained that "especially of late, there has been a growing tendency on the part of visitors not to pray or to sing praises, but to deliver speeches".[15] The remedy used on occasions when the speech would be inordinately long was the singing of a hymn to drown the speaker's voice.

Sometimes, however, a visitor would be called upon by the revivalist to say a word. One of these was K. Behesmilan, the Armenian minister. He urged the congregation to pray for his native land and spoke of the cruel persecution which Christians suffered at the hands of the Turks : he graphically related the story as to how the Turks had come to the house of a native preacher whom they persecuted; how the little children and wife of the preacher were cowering with fear and pleading for mercy; and how it was all in vain. "The Turk is so cruel", was his explanation of the callousness of men who would take no heed of the entreaties of the poor woman and the little ones. He then went on to describe how the preacher was deprived of limb after limb without flinching in his loyalty to the Saviour; each time he was tested as torture followed torture, until he was ultimately flayed alive, and even at the very last he triumphantly gloried in his Saviour.[16] Fervent intercession followed this statement; many in the congregation were in tears and strong men wept without restraint.

The visiting minister was not always a foreigner. Thomas

Darlington of Cardiff expressed his belief in the authenticity of the revival on account of its parallels with a Cornish revival he had witnessed. The revival "was touching everybody, and touching them in the right place". He went on to illustrate his point. He knew one miner who drank beer out of a teapot with his meals. During the Cornish revival that miner came to him and said, "The Lord has converted me, converted my wife, and converted the teapot."[17] The principal of Spurgeon's College, Dr. A. McCaig, was present at most of the Swansea meetings, not only to receive a blessing, but also to pass it on. Roberts' brief message to his students was, "Tell them to live very near to God. That is the best life—near to God".[18]

Triumphant progress

By the end of 1904 some 32,000 converts had been counted, mainly in South Wales.[19] In a pastoral letter on the revival, Bishop John Owen of Saint David's called for "an attitude of sympathy, watchfulness, and prayer", and continued :

"This movement, which has suddenly brought spiritual realities to the forefront of public interest in Wales, calls for our sincere sympathy. I know from my personal intercourse with the clergy that there has been among us a growing sense of our need of deeper spiritual life . . . Watchfulness, on more sides than one, follows from our sympathy with the revival. (1) First of all we have to watch against irreverence . . . (2) The divine purpose of religious feeling is revealed to be the formation of Christian character, the production of 'the fruit of the Spirit'. Religious feeling is, therefore, a spiritual means for a practical purpose, not a spiritual luxury for indulgence, much less a spectacle . . . (3) We have to be watchful . . . to learn 'what the Spirit saith unto the Churches' through the revival. Three things may be singled out for our special attention :— (a) . . . the important place which Holy Scripture assigns to the priesthood of the laity, and to the demand for personal service which our Lord makes upon every member of His Church . . . (b) . . . the divine institution and the responsibilities of the Christian ministry . . . (c) . . . that spiritual power comes only from the Holy Spirit . . . It follows . . . that our present attitude should be especially an attitude of prayer . . . The power of the Holy Spirit is imparted to the Church of Christ in proportion to the reality and purity of its prayers."[20]

These timely words carried weight, providing as they did a sane and necessary corrective to the extremes of both hostility and sensationalism.

Apart from a break at his home in Loughor over Christmas, Roberts' meetings continued into the New Year. There seemed to be no abatement in the spiritual power of the meetings or the physical health of the revivalist. Writing to D. M. Phillips early in January 1905 he could say, "More strength is given unto me (1) physically and spiritually in these days, (2) more light, (3) faith, (4) love, and (5) wisdom . . . what a glorious life! Divine in its purity".[21] A similarly triumphant note permeates his letter to Sidney Evans at the end of that month :

"Peace be to you! May you be filled with Grace, Joy, and Wisdom. God in you, round about and before you; a Strong Tower, your Strength, Light, and a fiery flame within you. May success attend you! Heaven send the heavy showers upon you day and night! May your face be radiant with the Joy of Heaven. Like Moses, may you be allowed to go into the bright cloud to the God of gods, and like him, to speak the *Words of God*. The Evil One *often* tempts me to speak *my own* words; but, Praise Him! the Holy Spirit through His wisdom overcomes me, overcomes the world, and the Devil, in all his wiles; and so He gives me words and ideas that answer to the need of the crowd. This gives me trouble; I know not whether it troubles you.

"Another way that he has is to try to get me to push myself *to the front*. But! Oh! that would be a curse to me, would spoil the work, and rob God of glory. Really, is it not important to keep ourselves in the background? I remember how in one meeting a voice said to me, 'Cry out the word "Judgement! Judgement!!"' But, Praise be to the Spirit, I was prevented from doing so, else 'Mr. Self' would have manifested himself at once. Another thing: I thought it was necessary to make use at all times of the things I had from the Holy Spirit. But that is a mistake. He has plenty of variety. But we must take care to be in His hands, body and soul."[22]

Within a week, however, there came a change of sufficient magnitude to influence both his spiritual discernment and his physical state.

Virulent opposition

The immediate cause of the change was an attack on his motives and methods by a Congregational minister, Peter Price. This appeared in the correspondence columns of the *Western Mail* on January 31st, and initiated a protracted and heated public debate, although Roberts himself took no part in it. Price claimed that there were two revivals, one true and the other false. The former had been in progress for as long as two years, his own church at Dowlais having been blessed with an increase of some hundreds in the previous five or six months. The Evan Roberts movement, on the other hand, was "a sham . . . a mockery, a blasphemous travesty of the real thing". The former, "the gloriously real revival", was of

God and its fire was heavenly; the latter, "the bogus Revival", was of man and its fire was "false" and "fleshly".[23]

The sympathy of the people lay with Roberts. The abusive letter had been signed, "Peter Price (B.A. Hons.), Mental and Moral Sciences Tripos, Cambridge (late of Queens' College, Cambridge)", and had included an oblique reference to the revivalist's lack of intellectual attainment. Price's derision on this score smacked of jealousy, and the people would have recalled that Peter and John were "un-learned and ignorant men" by the academic standards of the Jerusalem council. Fundamentally, however, their support of Roberts stemmed from a conviction of the authenticity of his revival work.

Consequently, while he did not make an appearance until the afternoon meeting at Troed-y-rhiw near Merthyr the next day, the congregation had passed in the morning "a resolution of strong protest" against Price's strictures.[24] A week later his hostile broadside had evoked a similar protest from the theological students at Bangor. They had read the criticisms with "much alarm", and expressed surprise that a minister of the gospel should have taken such an attitude. Their state-ment concluded: "we object to the tone of the whole letter and its personal references as tending to harm a movement which has brought immense blessing to our land."[25] Price received many letters, some offensive and some commendatory. Not one, however, discussed seriously the points at issue.

Basically, these were theological rather than psychological. Price had two main objections. He utterly repudiated Roberts' claim to being under the immediate, sustained control of the Holy Spirit, and dismissed the physical manifestations, from agony to ecstasy, as sheer exhibitionism. Neither pheno-menon was new in the history of the Church, and while the first implied the possibility of delusion, the second raised the question of excesses.

An immediacy of the Spirit's direction and control was evident in the experience of the apostles after the day of Pentecost. Peter's encounter with Ananias and Sapphira (Acts 5 : 1-11), and Paul's skirmish with Elymas the sorcerer (Acts 13 : 8-12) are notable instances of this. Nor was it confined to the apostolic circles, witness Philip the evangelist's digression to deal with the Ethiopian eunuch (Acts 8 : 26-40), and Ananias' reluctant ministrations to the newly converted Saul of Tarsus (Acts 9 : 10-19). With the consolidation of a formal and liturgical tradition, and the rise of an exclusive priestly caste to minister in the Church, succeeding generations did not always tolerate or even recognize the rule of the Spirit. As early as the second half of the second century those who did were reviled as heretics, their distinctive teachings were grossly caricatured, and their persons were treated as second-class citizens of the kingdom of God.

They were referred to as Montanists, after their leader Montanus, and their teachings have been summarized as follows : First, a strong faith in the Holy Spirit as the promised Paraclete, present as a heavenly power in the Church of the day; secondly, specially the belief that the Holy Spirit was manifesting Himself supernaturally at that day through entranced prophets and prophetesses; and thirdly, an inculcation of a specially stern and exacting standard of Christian morality and discipline on the strength of certain teachings of these prophets.[26]

Although the movement originated in the province of Phrygia in Asia Minor about A.D.150, its influence spread to Rome and North Africa, and lasted into the sixth century.[27] Its principal theological exponent was the renowned Tertullian, who charged one of its opposers with doing "a two-fold service to the devil at Rome by driving away prophecy and bringing in heresy (patripassianism), or by putting to flight the Holy Spirit and crucifying God the Father."[28]

Now and again in the history of the Church the spiritual descendants of Montanus have appeared, only to be maligned and persecuted for their emphasis upon the relationship between the Holy Spirit and the believer. Nevertheless it has always been difficult for mere human nature to distinguish between the decree of the Spirit and the desire of self, and even more difficult to submit to the former when it was in conflict with the latter. Wales had witnessed these things in the two previous centuries. In the eighteenth century Howel Harris had been censured by, and virtually excommunicated from, the Methodist ranks for this very reason, although the issue was confused at the time by other considerations. In his defence Harris claimed, "My spiritual light in private and preaching even had on them become a burden, and they called me a pope and trampled on my authority. They had also left the teaching of the Spirit to lean on and study books".[29] One of the leading instruments in the Welsh revival of 1859, Humphrey Jones, claimed a direct revelation from the Holy Spirit. Its purpose was to vindicate his mission in a hard, unresponsive town, but the outcome brought him only remorse.[30]

A turning point

In the case of Evan Roberts the instances where he might be suspected of delusion are remarkably scarce. With the appearance of Price's unqualified and virulent opposition, Roberts seemed to depend more and more on direct, Spirit-inspired perception both as to the conduct of the meetings and the content of his messages. During the days which followed the appearance of Price's attack, hardly a meeting passed without Roberts detecting the presence of an "obstacle" of one kind or another.[31] H. Elvet Lewis wrote of this period : "He was more and more given to locate hindrances at his meetings, and almost to name the hinderers. It was the growth of these practices that led to some most unhappy incidents both by way of attack and defence."[32]

The French observer, Professor Henri Bois, also saw the Peter Price controversy as a turning-point in the revival :

"Roberts ignored these attacks, nevertheless they had their effect on him, for he now became more passionately concerned about immediate revelations from the Holy Spirit. This came to a head with the extraordinary incident at Cwmavon, on the 21st of February, 1905. During the meeting Roberts cried out in agony that there was a damned soul present in the meeting; the congregation began to pray, but Roberts stopped them, saying that there was no point in praying, for this soul was finally damned."[33]

As early as February 3rd Roberts had been obliged, on doctor's advice, to take a rest "in consequence of an attack of nervous prostration".[34] On the day following the Cwmavon meeting he refused to fulfil his engagement at Briton Ferry and retired for seven days' silence.

According to the revivalist there were two reasons. One was his impending visit to Liverpool, for which he "must leave Wales without money", the other reason was "the divine command", actions based upon Luke 10 :4 and Ezekiel 3 :24-26 respectively.[35] Later, he claimed the reasons were not physical or mental, but the silence was a sign from the Lord : "as your tongue was bound for seven days, even so Satan shall be bound for seven times".[36] While the decision appeared arbitrary it gave him much-needed physical and mental respite, and probably saved him from a spiralling tendency to excesses.

These would have brought about the ruin of the revivalist and the eclipse of his usefulness.

Excesses in evidence

Excesses were in evidence, however, among the revival congregations, as in every period of awakening in the history of the Church. Christ's parable of the sower was a warning of the appearance of counterfeit fruit (Luke 8 :4-15). Simon the magician (Acts 8 :9-24) and the seven sons of Sceva (Acts 19 :13-17) were instances in New Testament times of those whose interest in spiritual things was entirely superficial.

Physical prostrations and contortions were quite common under the ministries of George Whitefield and John Wesley. Whitefield's initial alarm at these powerful manifestations was modified into caution by Wesley's observations :

"I had an opportunity to talk with him of those outward signs which had so often accompanied the inward work of God. I found his objections were chiefly founded on gross misrepresentations of matters of fact. But the next day he had an opportunity of informing himself better : for no sooner had he begun (in the application of his sermon) to invite all sinners to believe in Christ, than four persons sunk down close to him, almost in the same moment. One of them lay without either sense or motion; a second trembled exceedingly; the third had strong convulsions all over his body, but made no noise, unless by groans; the fourth, equally convulsed, called upon God, with strong cries and tears. From this time, I trust, we shall all suffer God to carry on His own work in the way that pleaseth Him."[37]

An American contemporary of theirs, Jonathan Edwards, was obliged to face the dangers of counterfeit physical manifestations among his own people. His exceptionally useful treatise, *Some thoughts concerning the present revival of religion,* was directed towards correcting misunderstanding as well as misbehaviour in it.

To answer Price's charge in this respect it is sufficient to note the title of the third section in the first part of Edwards' work, "We should distinguish the good from the bad and not judge of the whole by a part". No one discerned the issues more clearly in 1904 than the influential and able minister, E. Keri Evans. Speaking of his ministry during the revival he recalls :

"I was invited to meetings up and down the land and proclaimed chiefly, 'Conviction is not conversion' . . . adding, 'nor is awakening, repentance' . . . there were many . . who had been on the crest of a wave of jubilation for wellnigh a whole year, and when the jubilation subsided sought to regain it by artificial means, not realizing that the Holy Spirit works through the imagination and the emotion to the conscience to produce repentance, and through the conscience to the will in order to lead to conversion."[38]

If Roberts by his example and methods gave prominence to the element of feeling in spiritual experience, he could not be charged with advocating or stimulating an infectious emotionalism. He recognized the pitfalls and was sensitive enough to identify them : "When there comes a pause in the services, then there is a danger of someone swinging the pendulum instead of raising the weights."[39]

Increased difficulties

The February meetings had been attended with severe trial and difficulty for Roberts. There seemed to be no respite from the spiritual opposition which he encountered in them.

The successful progress of his ministry had reached its climax in the middle of January; its arrest and comparatively sudden decline can be traced to the Dowlais meetings and to the open hostility of one of the town's ministers. No small part of the responsibility for the eclipse of Roberts' usefulness must be laid at the door of Peter Price. That his scorn adversely affected the revivalist is beyond doubt; that it altered the course of events seems likely. In addition, it drew attention to the more peripheral characteristics of the movement. This in turn vitiated subsequent assessment of the revival and gave rise to confused thinking about the issues involved.

The only redeeming feature in the entire Price episode was Roberts' refusal to be drawn into argument. Not a single word was issued by him in defence at the time. Even eight years later his comments on the revival's setbacks were confined to general principles and avoided all appearance of personal rancour : "The mistake at the time of the Revival in Wales in 1904 was to become occupied with the *effects* of the Revival, and not to watch and pray in protecting and guarding the cause of Revival."[40]

In the intervening period before his work at Liverpool Roberts divided the time between his home and the familiar Cardiganshire scene. It was as if he desired the heavenly flame to purge him from the dross of past failure and at the same time rekindle his own flickering lamp of ardour. It was not to be. At Blaenannerch he was constrained to expose publicly as a hindrance to the meeting a person present whose name had been "revealed" to him, while at the New Quay meeting he was faced with no little difficulty.[41] He returned to Loughor obsessed with thoughts of obedience and the divine fire. Before departing for Liverpool only one sacrifice remained. He gave away all his money.

Visit to Liverpool

News of the revival had of course preceded Evan Roberts at Liverpool. It had come not only through the medium of the press but also by the personal report of visiting speakers from the revival areas. As early as January 1905 the Welsh churches particularly were in a ferment over the news, and longed that the revival would spill over into Liverpool. A contemporary diarist speaks of the revival in those early days of 1905 as "growing bigger in men's minds", and the Welsh chapels in the city "smouldering although they have not broken out into flame as have the chapels in Wales".[42]

The object of Roberts' mission was almost exclusively this Welsh community. Throughout the period of his stay—nearly three weeks—the congregations were large, the people responsive, and the meetings fruitful, the total reckoning being about 750 converts.[43] The Liverpool crowds were supplemented by visitors from North Wales and the Midlands, all eager to receive and return with the blessing. A revival committee consisted of the executive of the Liverpool Welsh Free Church Council, with John Williams, minister of the Calvinistic Methodist church in Prince's Road, and Henry Jones as joint secretaries, the former especially giving Roberts unqualified support. Williams was enthusiastic enough to meet Roberts, his sister Mary, Annie Davies, and D. M. Phillips at Chester in order to accompany them for the remainder of the journey.[44] Such was the impact of Roberts' coming that a civic reception was given in his honour by the Lord Mayor.

The first meeting was held, appropriately, in Williams' church, also the venue of other revival meetings. Indeed, according to one estimate, "some of the most effective meetings" were held here, "even though there was no great increase in the membership as a result" of the revival.[45] At the initial meetings emphasis was laid by Roberts on obedience, preparing a place for the Holy Spirit, and the duty of forgiveness. Subsequent to these three, however, the meetings were almost all attended with difficulties of some kind or another.

Roberts caused no little consternation on more than one occasion by naming ministers among the hindrances to the meetings.[46] At other meetings he complained of the presence of a "scoffer", stopped someone praying on account of the "great disobedience" he felt in their midst, and could not read the Bible because "there was some great obstacle" present.[47] A packed Sun Hall, "a huge building used only for religious services . . . capable of accommodating 6,000" witnessed tense drama. Roberts had stopped the singing and allowed only prayer, when he suddenly stopped the service, saying in Welsh and English, "there is one English friend in this meeting who tries to hypnotise me this very moment". He continued :

"Will you leave the building at once or ask the Lord to forgive you? God will not be mocked. We don't come here to play. We come here to worship the Lord . . . There has been too much playing with sacred things. People come to the Lord's temple to play with things which have cost divine blood. It is time they were swept away or brought in to assist, instead of obstructing."

The truth of his assertion was later publicly acknowledged by a hypnotist appearing at the Lyric theatre.[48]

Another notable incident concerned the newly-formed Free Church of the Welsh. This was a secession from the Welsh Calvinistic Methodist church at Chatham Street under its minister, W. O. Jones. The denomination had deposed him from office in 1901 on the grounds of drunkenness, and by April 1905 five churches had been opened belonging to this splinter group. One of these, the Donaldson Street church, later claimed to be the place where revival influences were first felt in Liverpool.[49]

In the public meeting concerned, Roberts had been in intense agony from the time of his arrival. Eventually he got up to make the statements which created a great sensation at the time :

"God committed this message to me many days ago, but only tonight is it to be disclosed. The message relates to the Free Church of the Welsh. This is the message. Do as you like with it. It comes direct from God :— 'The foundations of the Church are not on the Rock. The foundations of the Church are not on the Rock' . . . I would rather not have delivered it, but somebody must say it. O God, give strength to these people . . . I knew this was going to be a terrible service. I felt too weak almost to walk in from the vestry, but it is all over now. Thank God, peace and unity are still possible."[50]

Towards the end of the mission at Liverpool Roberts remained silent in the pulpit for considerable periods, emphasising both by brief comment and manner his belief in the priority of prayer : "We may sing all night without saving. It is prayer that tells, that saves, and that brings heaven down among us. Pray, friends, pray."[51]

Obstacles, scoffers, interruptions, disorder, the hypnotist, the Free Church of the Welsh, Roberts' health and his silence, all these things account for the fact that the Liverpool mission is remembered for its incidents rather than its achievements. Contemporary newspaper reporters, however, were impressed by factors other than the sensational. One gave prominence to the content of his message : "Whatever his co-workers may have done, he himself never inveighs against specific forms of evil. He never mentions drunkenness, gambling, immorality, commercial dishonesty, or social injustice. If a man gets right with God and gets the love of Christ in his heart, he cannot live a sinful life, but must perforce be a better man and a better citizen. That conviction is the pole-star by which he steers clear of many difficult problems and many unprofitable controversies. One cannot help feeling that in this avoidance of political and social grievances he has carefully studied the methods of the Master, and this is, I think, one of the secrets of his great success."[52]

Another, writing for an avowedly satirical paper, acknowledged that his prejudices had received a decisively fatal blow : "I was thus prepared to meet a weird, irresponsible fanatic, who could so play on the feelings of a people, already by nature emotional, and of necessity simple and illiterate, that the hysterical side would be kept uppermost, and the good to be derived from his ministrations a doubtful and transient quality. There is nothing of all this about Evan Roberts."[53]

The Liverpool mission can only be understood by reference to the spiritual forces of good and evil engaged in deadly conflict. The Welsh churches of the city were only the arena of the mighty struggle for supremacy. Far too many spectators riveted their attention on the idiosyncrasies, the horrors, the gory details of the battle, seemingly unaware of the forces involved. They little realized, still less sympathized with, the fierce agony which Roberts experienced on that spiritual battlefield. To him, at any rate, Liverpool was yet another victory for the Lord of hosts. "The power of God which broke forth in Wales, with all the marks of the days of Pentecost, has been checked and kept back from going on to its fullest purpose, by the same influx of evil spirits as met the Lord Christ on earth, and the Apostles of the early Church; with the difference that the inroad of the powers of darkness found the Christians of the twentieth century, with few exceptions, unable to recognize, and deal with them."[54]

The final meetings, one at Liverpool and the other at Birkenhead, were more subdued. John Williams admitted the concern of many supporters over the revivalist's health and read the certified statement of physicians after medical examination : "We find him mentally and physically quite sound. He is suffering from the effects of overwork, and we consider it advisable that he should have a period of rest."[55] Consequently, accompanied by the same two ladies and John Williams, Roberts left next day for Betws-y-coed.

Ministry in North Wales

Although Roberts spent more than two months in North Wales his ministry was not as crucial or successful as in his native Glamorgan. The main reason for this was the rapid spread of the revival independently of his personal appearance. R. B. Jones had held missions in Anglesey in January 1905 with eminent success. His message was directed essentially to Christians and centred on the holiness of God. Speaking at Amlwch on Isaiah 6, when he "came to the words telling of the *'live coals from off the altar'*—the cleansing fire from the place where blood was shed, Calvary—suddenly, without one word of explanation, the Holy Spirit so unveiled the truth that the majority of the large congregation of twelve hundred people simultaneously sprang to their feet shouting 'Diolch Iddo' (Thanks be to Him), whilst the glory of the Lord so shone upon the pulpit that the missioner fled to the vestry completely overcome".[56]

Roberts' meetings were sympathetically and fully reported in the North Wales press, *Yr Herald Cymraeg* particularly giving extensive coverage. By the 5th of May he could write to D. M. Phillips, "My mind is clearer, the memory is revived, and the imagination ready to wing its flight to the distant country". To his friends he wrote on a postcard :

> The mountains are high—my hope is higher;
> The mountains are strong—my faith is stronger;
> The mountains will depart—my God, never.[57]

Most of June was spent in Anglesey with mixed fortunes. Little success attended his meetings at Menai Bridge and Brynsiencyn, while other places had experienced the heavenly fire before his coming. During the revival years the Calvinistic Methodist churches alone counted an addition of nearly 2,000 communicant members.[58]

In July he visited Caernarvon and Bala, maintaining his distinctive methods and emphases. The *Traethodydd* of the same month reprinted, under the title "A Message for God's Church", an article by Roberts which had appeared in the *Homiletic Review*. Its burden was Roberts' desire to attribute the whole of the revival's achievements to God alone; the revivalist was merely an instrument, no new or distinctive doctrine was promulgated, and he had no technique, only an entire dependence on God. Yet more blessing would attend the churches "if they learned the lesson of obedience to the Holy Spirit".

Roberts spent the end of the month at Llandrindod, and in a letter written at the time the germ of a new emphasis appears, that of watchfulness : "If ever there was need for the church of God to be watchful, it is more so today than ever. 'Watch.' This verse is ever present with me, 'Watch and pray.' "[59] Reporting a meeting with him early in September H. Elvet Lewis wrote : "He had no programme for the future, immediate or distant, he was waiting. 'These are days of struggle, of great struggle to me', he remarked. He referred to the appeals that come to him from all parts of the world, and said sadly, 'The devil is pulling very hard . . .' So we left him to his lonely struggles of soul . . . He has been spending the weeks since in almost unbroken retirement."[60] The revivalist had been thrust into another phase of the revival, that of the conflict for its consolidation.

CHAPTER 9

WIDESPREAD ACHIEVEMENTS

WHILE Evan Roberts was the most prominent figure in the revival the work was not limited to human instrumentality. In those days to hear of the revival movement in South Wales was sufficient stimulus to set many churches praying for a similiar operation of the Holy Spirit in their own midst. The pattern usually followed was to hold a series of prayer meetings in which the young people almost invariably took a prominent part, until the heavenly influences intensified and the control of the meetings was beyond human determination. Such was the case, for instance, at the widely separated Tanygrisiau, Merionethshire, and Pentwyn, Carmarthenshire.[1] Often the influence would spread through the instrumentality of church courts, as in North Cardiganshire through a presbytery meeting held at Pen-llwyn in December 1904.[2] These meetings proved very powerful, and the delegates returned to their various churches determined to spread the divine fire. In this way the revival progressed rapidly and irresistibly throughout the Principality.

In terms of numbers, the Calvinistic Methodists received an added 24,000 into membership, the Wesleyans over 4,000, the Congregationalists, 26,500 in 1904-1905. The Anglican and Baptist churches brought the total figure to Roberts' visionary 100,000. The fourth pamphlet of *The Religious Revival in Wales* appeared in March 1905, and listed a total for Wales of 83,936, the spiritual harvest in the north being largely counted in later months.[3]

146

Movements in the British Isles

The revival was not as widespread or general in England. A "revival map" printed in the fifth number of the *Western Mail* pamphlets shows a heavily shaded Wales and Cornwall, and lightly shaded counties of Cumberland, Durham, Gloucestershire, Hampshire, Lancashire, Middlesex, Northumberland, Warwickshire, Westmorland and Yorkshire. In December 1905 Roberts visited Bristol at the invitation of T. Ferrier Hulme, and his "address was followed by a great outburst of spontaneous prayer and testimony, in which scores of people joined very fervently. Subsequently, scores rose to testify their desire to consecrate themselves to the Master's service".[4]

In the north of England, at Hirst, Northumberland, enthusiastic meetings were being conducted by a miner, William Willis. Several hundred converts were reported within a few days, with the people parading the streets in great agitation.[5] At Douglas, Isle of Man, the work of the Salvation Army was being eminently blessed, some forty converts being reported in January 1905. Further south on the island in Ballasalla there were an estimated fifty converts in the same period.[6]

Two months later a "revival party" travelled from South Wales to Glasgow and experienced much success.[7] Further north in the Orkneys there were reports of "a gracious visitation", and its impact was such that the reporters claimed that there had been "no movement like it within the memory of any one living".[8]

Seth Joshua visited the General Assembly of the Presbyterian Church in Ireland of 1905 reporting on the Welsh revival, and two Irish evangelists, Billy Spence and John McNeill, exercised fruitful ministries in Belfast during the revival period.[9]

Worldwide effects

It was inevitable that the impact of the revival should be felt among the Welsh exiles scattered throughout the world, notably on the mission fields of Madagascar and India, but also in Patagonia. H. Elvet Lewis says of the former that "the revival was reproduced almost in facsimile", and of the latter that the story of the revival was "as wonderful as anything in the homeland".[10]

On hearing news of the Welsh work the missionaries in Madagascar solemnly pledged together to pray for a similar visitation. As the divine influences began to break upon them they recognised the parallels to the Welsh work : "There were physical manifestations like those seen in Wales . . . there were great searchings of heart and confessions of sin, manifest repentance and many conversions."[11] The religious stirrings experienced in Patagonia among the Welsh colonists during the latter half of 1905 were very strong.[12]

In North America the Welsh churches sought revival blessing in prayer on hearing accounts of the work in Wales; Plymouth and Wilkesbarre (Pennsylvania), together with Fairhaven and West Pawlet (New York) are especially mentioned.[13]

The revival could not be contained within the narrow limits of the Welsh settlements. As early as February 1905 the writer of an editorial in the *Christian Advocate* felt that "the evidences of the coming of a general religious revival, which shall move the whole country from border to border, are accumulating . . . there is something more this year".[14] Consequently, when in 1906 Seth Joshua visited the North American scene, the revival phenomena were as powerful as those experienced in Wales, and for many that year was "a year of revival, a year of the Holy Ghost".[15]

Over the border in Mexico City accounts of the Welsh revival stirred many of the English-speaking community to prayer, and 1905 proved to be a time of quickening in their midst.[16]

Europe

Continental Europe was also aware of this divine visitation in the Principality. David Lloyd-George spoke of its influence in places as far away as Paris and Naples.[17] Visitors from France had returned home with renewed evangelistic fervour :

"We would not magnify unduly the influence which the Welsh Revival had on our Churches . . . But the fact remains, that some of us have received an impulse at those wonderful meetings which made, as it were, the whole of Wales blaze in the sight of the world, in that year 1905. And through men who brought some of that fire from Wales, evangelistic campaigns have been conducted, in places where no such thing had ever been witnessed; conversions have taken place in many towns and villages."[18]

The French Home Office delegated an experienced medical psychiatrist to gather evidence "as part of an investigation being undertaken by the French Public Health Department concerning the effect of religious excitement in France on those suffering from nervous instability". The resulting French publication was sympathetic and objective.[19]   A second French publication on the 1904 revival was by a theologian of the Reformed Church and was similarly favourable. "I profoundly believe that God is really, considerably and undeniably at work in the Welsh Revival. The Spirit of God is here."[20]

T. B. Barratt, a Cornishman who in 1902 had founded the Oslo City Mission, corresponded with Evan Roberts in 1905.[21]

He had been editor of the Mission's paper *Byposten* since 1904, and in a January 1905 issue of that magazine had listed "the conditions of being blessed, set down by the revival in Wales".[22] In a book on the Welsh revival published the same year in Oslo, attention was drawn particularly to the lack of liturgical order in the meetings, and their being in the control of the inspiration of the moment.[23]

The revivalist activities of a young converted sailor, Albert Lunde, made him, in the eyes of many, an Oslo counterpart to Evan Roberts. He was reckoned to be "as simple in his ways and speech", but ecclesiastical dignitaries were sympathetic and showed deep interest in his work. Although the sensationalism of the Welsh movement was notably absent, an overall assessment claimed that "nothing outside of Wales compares with the work which is still in progress in Norway". Its effects were widespread, and its results were spiritually and morally beneficial among all classes of people throughout the land.[24]

Neighbouring Sweden also caught the spiritual flame early in 1905, "signs of revival" becoming evident after the Christian community had "heard of the great blessings" in Wales.[25] The awakening in Denmark began in the autumn of the same year, and continued throughout the winter, its main instrument being the Lutheran Inner Mission.[26]

An extraordinary awakening in the Ruhr in Germany followed the return of a tent campaign evangelist, Jakob Vetter, from his visit to the scenes of the Welsh revival. The work spread to many parts of the land and resulted in the setting up of Christian societies for various trades, professions, and industries.[27]

On a more ecclesiastically formal level, the Synod of the Belgian Christian Missionary Church, working among coal miners, altered its agenda to consider reports of the revival in

Wales.[28]   In the Balkans there was spiritual quickening among the evangelical minorities of Hungary and Bulgaria during 1905.   The extent of this movement of God's Spirit was declared to be "widespread", and its progress followed the familiar pattern of extended prayer meetings, confession of sin, and conversions.[29]

Africa

Various parts of the African continent were also stirred, from Algeria to the Cape.   It was Reuben Saillens, the French evangelist, who gave news of the revival to audiences of 1,200 to 2,000 in Algiers, so that by 1906 he could report "the most encouraging time ever known" in the capital.[30]

Prayer meetings and conferences multiplied in great profusion in South Africa on hearing of the Welsh revival. Attention was especially focussed on the town of Villiersdorp, some fifty miles from Cape Town.   Here the Methodists reported unusual revival activity in the midsummer of 1905, and at a Christian Endeavour meeting in July there were "indescribable happenings".   These included intense conviction of sin, simultaneous praying, and a solemn preoccupation with God throughout the community.   As well as numerous conversions, the movement resulted in a transformed society and invigorated missionary enterprise.[31]

Australasia

From the Christian journals of Australasia it is evident that news of the Welsh revival created great interest in Australia.[32].   Reports reached New Zealand early in 1905, stirring up interest in such places as Wanganui and the mining district of Waihi.   "Many of the salient features of the wonderful Welsh revival" were evident in these spontaneous awakenings.[33]

Asia

The quickening of spiritual life was also experienced in widely separated areas of the vast continent of Asia. Manchuria had already witnessed a measure of revival in 1903. It was a movement which "spread simultaneously through almost every district, humbling, gladdening, establishing churches, remote and near." It issued in a prayer movement through much of south and west China which continued into 1904. Missionaries and nationals alike were later encouraged to more fervent prayer "that China might experience a similarly gracious visitation of the Holy Spirit as has recently been seen in Wales".[34]

By the end of 1906 reports from China Inland Mission workers on the field showed that the prayers had been abundantly answered : "China also has had its revivals this year, especially in the north. It is significant that here and in Shanghai and Canton, the initiative has been so often and so largely Chinese. These revivals have been marked by a wholly unusual conviction of sin and by great anxiety for the conversion of friends and neighbours."[35]

As in Manchuria, so also in Korea, there was an initial wave of revival in 1903.[36] Revival movements in Korea from 1903-1907 benefited tremendously from the adoption by missionaries in 1890 of indigenous principles of missionary strategy. These had been advocated by Dr. John L. Nevius of China and emphasised thorough Bible training for nationals and a self-supporting church administration.[37]

The impact of the Welsh revival on North Korea was such that churches were crowded and many conversions were registered. "It was described as a spreading fire, a continuous religious awakening", and more conversions were reported throughout the country in 1905 than in any previous year.[38]

The climax, however, came in 1907 after a winter of powerful awakenings. Confession of sin, reconciliation between enemies, restitution of goods, sustained and fervent prayer meetings, and evangelistic zeal were the result.[39]

India

Nowhere were the revival manifestations repeated with such similarity and intensity as on the Indian mission field of the Calvinistic Methodists. Located in the North East of the country, Assam had been the particular province of Welsh Presbyterian missionary labour for over sixty years. A weekly prayer meeting had been started early in 1903 to pray explicitly for an outpouring of the Holy Spirit. On hearing reports of the Welsh work the desire for a time of reviving deepened, and in certain parts of the field many set themselves to pray each night for it.

The Cherrapoonjee Assembly of February 1905 proved a great blessing, an earnest of things to come. It was said of the delegates, "These Khassies are praying and weeping in the houses the whole time".[40] Prayer meetings mushroomed throughout the field as a result of the Assembly, its delegates having returned to pour fresh fuel on an already smouldering fire. In March some of the churches were studying John 1 :33 in Sunday School and considering the baptism of the Spirit, with the possible hindrances to its being received. At the close of that solemn meeting someone prayed, "O Lord, break our hardened hearts. We are ashamed that we are so hard, especially since Christ has done so much for us". Many were broken and the sound of weeping became quite general.[41]

It was at a presbytery meeting some days later that the full impact of the revival was felt. Much prayer had been offered on behalf of the festival and there was a keen sense of expectancy as the time approached. This was held at Pariong in the Mawphlang district and lasted three days. In their prayers the people desired an outpouring similar to that experienced in Wales. When these were in evidence they were immediately recognized to be parallel manifestations.

On the third day, after the usual preaching exercises, one of the leaders prayed for a special blessing before departing. This seemed to stimulate spontaneous, general prayer from numbers of people all at once, and the scene which followed was almost indescribable. "O God! pour out your Spirit upon us *now;* while you are blessing the people of Wales so richly, don't let us go away empty-handed." Simultaneously others started to pray, men and women, and it is difficult to say what happened then : many prayed; some cried out for mercy; some of the men fainted; almost the entire congregation wept, and some praised God. Then someone began to sing, and the verse was repeated time and time again, until some were nearly dancing with joy.[42]

A correspondent wrote at the time : "The Revival has commenced in earnest here, confessing, singing and praying and all in tears, and determined to live henceforth more worthy of our Lord Jesus Christ. It is now past midnight, and several are now in the chapel singing and praying".[43]

The blessing radiated from that presbytery over a wide area. At Cherrapoonjee, when a girl began to pray for her uncles, all the people began to scream and cry for pardon. "Nothing would pacify the people, one started one hymn, and another, another, but it only made them worse, scores crying for forgiveness, confessing sins against themselves . . . while this went on the heathen came running in and then ran out, then in again, not understanding what had taken place . . . at first the women seemed more affected than the men, but now the men and women were similarly moved."[44]

The powerful influences were not confined to the meetings

or church buildings. Mrs. John Roberts, one of the missionaries on the field, who was later to tell the story of the revival, relates an incident in one of the native women's homes. "Once while conducting family worship the Holy Spirit fell powerfully upon her and her nephew, so that they jumped and danced, all the while praising God for his grace. The neighbours ran into the house and discovered the whole family singing and rejoicing in the Lord."[45]

The manner of the revival's spreading is typified in the case of Lawburtyn, a village some 25 miles from Mawphlang. Some of the Christians had been to a preaching festival where the Spirit's visitation had been especially powerful. Back home the following day, "they seemed to be hungering for the blessing, and before long a number of them began to wend their steps to the Chapel to pray secretly, but when they found others of the same mind, they joyfully united in prayer and they soon felt the Divine Presence with them so that the leading men of the Church were trembling with emotion as they called upon God. The special prayer meeting in the evening was attended by all the Christians and by a large number of the heathen. The prayers were remarkable for their fervour and there was a general confession of sins before the Lord and many were silently weeping".[46]

By May the influence had intensified further. "On Sunday, May 7th, the whole day was devoted to prayer. After the early morning service, seven of the brethren remained behind to pray, they felt that they could not leave the place without the blessing which they sought. They prayed one after another and then they were so overcome by their feelings that they found themselves all praying aloud at the same time. The heathen living near the chapel heard and came running in and the place was soon filled. They had glorious services all day, and when all the meetings were over and the congregation had departed, nine Christians remained behind again for more prayer, and strange to say others came running back so that the Chapel was again crowded, many non-Christians being present. It was at that time that a strange bright light filled the place and the mighty power of the Spirit came upon them. Oh! what a scene it was! the whole place was in apparent confusion, some praying aloud, others confessing their sins, many of the heathen in agony appealing to God for pardon, some even fainted, so great was the power. It was a pleasure to hear some of the older Christians praising God and shouting, 'The Church now lives! The Church now lives!'.''[47]

Throughout the progress of the work the leaders showed a remarkable "willingness to follow the lead of the Spirit", even though the sight of physical prostrations, dancing, and wild excitement would have been previously repugnant to them.[48]

A second wave of pentecostal influence spread through the field in June. This manifested itself particularly in the quality of the singing and the expression of joy on the faces of the Christians. "The people sing not only with their voices, but with all their body, and why should not God's praise be expressed by hands and feet as well as by the tongue? It is easy to understand . . . why people on the day of Pentecost charged the apostles with being full of new wine."[49] According to one commentator, "the religious experiences of the natives were brought into closer conformity to those of the pristine church than had been the case in . . . Wales".[50]

During its first phase the revival was characterized by "penitential weeping and sobbing, the whole congregation in tears, confessing their sin, agonizing in prayer for mercy, pleading for salvation", but three months later a fulness of joy took possession of the people.[51] The children, too, experienced the same emotions, at one time filling the church with their cries when nothing could comfort them, and later singing in exultation while they waved their hymn books, when none could stop them,

> *The love that Jesus had for me*
> *To suffer on the cruel tree,*
> *That I a ransomed soul might be*
> *Is more than tongue can tell.*[52]

The children continued to show zeal and enthusiasm for some time after the revival had generally declined.

The course of the work in India showed it to be clearly a movement of God's Spirit of immense proportions and lasting benefit. One of the native Christians summed up its fruit in three ways: a more fervent unity and love, a desire to be free of financial debt, and a greater desire to extend Christ's kingdom.[53] Its relationship to the Welsh revival can hardly be questioned. Although it issued in the consolidation of an indigenous work, its stimulus had come from the 'mother church'. The same mission field experienced further revivals in subsequent years, in 1913, 1919, and 1935, bringing the membership of the church in Lushai (the most southerly sector of the field) from a mere 32 in 1904 to over 103,000 in 1954. For some twenty years the majority of new missionaries to the field had been blessed during the revival in Wales.[54]

Further south, on the east coast of India, the Canadian mission working in Telugu country witnessed revival in 1906. A missionary had sent to Ongole some leaflets describing the Welsh work. Its effect was to create a sense of expectancy and a desire for prayer. At the customary April gathering for workers and elders the interest shown appeared to be more solemn and intense than usual. The exercises of worship on the Sunday had been quiet and restrained, but during a season of prayer on the following day the flood-gates of revival were suddenly opened. One of the missionaries wrote : "The usual stoical mindedness of our Indian assembly was broken as by an earthquake. Every one present was shaken. One of the most quiet and retiring of our workers arose and, striking his breast, cried in Telugu in a loud voice, 'Holy Spirit! Holy Spirit!' Many others followed. For the first time at Ongole, the Holy Spirit of God was glimpsed in the act of convicting His people of sin".

The awakening radiated to other parts of the field as the workers returned to their stations. With the personal testimony of a missionary who had actually been in the midst of the revival in Wales the powerful manifestations of the work were intensified in July.[55]

In the south-west corner of India the saintly Amy Carmichael witnessed unprecedented scenes of revival among the unemotional Tamil people of Dohnavur. Her account of its beginnings in October, 1905, reflects the astonishment and wonder she felt at the time : "It was at the close of the morning service that the break came. The one who was speaking was obliged to stop, overwhelmed by a sudden realization of the inner force of things. It was impossible even to pray. One of the older lads in the boys' school began to try to pray, but he broke down, then another, then all together, the older lads chiefly at first. Soon many among the younger ones began to cry bitterly, and pray for forgiveness. It spread to the women . . . Soon the whole upper half of the church was on its face on the floor crying to God . . . oblivious of all others. The sound was like the sound of waves or strong wind in the trees . . . I had never heard of such a thing as this among Tamil people . . . By this time, the lower end of the church, the careless part of the congregation was staring at the other part, and talking and shouting excitedly, and the heathen rushed round the church and gazed in at the doors and windows. But nothing disturbed those who were praying, and that hurricane of prayer continued with one short break of a few minutes for over four hours".

There followed a considerable disruption, but a blessed one, in the routine of the community : "For the next fortnight life was apportioned for us much as it was for the apostles when they gave themselves continually to prayer and to the ministry of the Word. Everything else had to stand aside". And the results? "Looking back after nearly seven months of testing, we have enough true results to make us sing with all our hearts. Almost all our children were, I trust, out and out converted. Most of our workers were thoroughly revived. The bungalow servants were greatly blessed, several backsliders were restored. Many of the schoolboys were converted . . . In the village there were several notable conversions and the true Christians were quickened . . . It was as if veils were suddenly drawn aside, and Gethsemane and Calvary and the Powers of the world to come suddenly became intensely real." In conclusion she was able to say, "The result in our own lives has been, I think, a quickened power of expectation".[56]

Towards the close of the nineteenth century, Pandita Ramabai, converted daughter of a Brahman scholar, started an orphanage at Mukti in the Maharashtra area of West India. Having heard of the Welsh revival she organized prayer circles at the beginning of 1905. In June of that year the women and girls under her care experienced some of the more severe physical manifestations of revival power. At first these caused her great concern, but she learned to submit to the sovereign working of the Holy Spirit. In spite of the emotional character of the work, the converts were steadfast in bearing witness twenty years later.[57]

The overall results of the Indian awakenings of 1905 were summarized by the Christian and Missionary Alliance in this way : "The revival has given a new body of native evangelists and most of our native preachers have experienced a baptism of the Holy Ghost which has completely transformed their spirit and work".[58]

In many ways this assessment could be applied to the achievements of the post-1904 awakenings on most of the missionary fields. The worldwide impact of the 1904 revival in Wales was therefore a significant and substantial contribution to the advance of Christianity in the twentieth century. Only faithful nationals and indigenous churches could consolidate that advance.

CHAPTER 10

NOTABLE CHARACTERISTICS

A S might be expected, an influx of new people into the churches brought new life and zeal. The sale of Bibles soared, the Sunday Schools received fresh recruits, buildings were either enlarged or completely rebuilt. Family worship was set up for the first time in many homes. The prayer meetings were invigorated, many new ones started, and others established which continued for several years to be a prominent and beneficial feature of the life of the churches; Sir John Morris-Jones, a prominent Welsh literary figure, was impressed by "the gift of speech evident in some of the least likely. I never heard anything as powerful as the prayers of certain young men to whom I could credit no literary gift whatsoever".[1] The gift was born of spiritual enlightenment rather than educational attainment.

Social impact

The social impact of the revival became proverbial. The pit-ponies could no longer understand the miners' instructions because of the absence of oaths and curses. The most notable effect of the revival was the precipitous decline in drunkenness. At Llanfair in Anglesey all public houses except one were closed.[2] Convictions for drunkenness in Glamorgan fell from 10,528 in 1903 to 5,490 in 1906.[3] It was claimed that "three months of the revival had done more to sober the country than the temperance effort of many years".[4]

In its wider aspect D. M. Phillips summarized the effects in this way: "Prayer meetings are held in the trains, and many converts are made. The public-houses and beer clubs are empty; old debts are paid; jealousy vanishes; church and family feuds are healed; great drunkards, prize-fighters, and gamblers pray in the services, and give their testimony; the chapels throughout the populous valleys of Glamorganshire are full every night; all denominations have sunk their small differences, and co-operate as one body; and the huge processions along the streets send a thrill of terror through the vilest sinners . . . The Revival is the topic in all spheres and amongst all sections of society; and strong people are overwhelmed by reading the newspaper accounts of it".[5]

The vices of that semi-Victorian era might seem a trifle naïve to the sophisticated society of subsequent generations. Evil has many faces, but its variety does not atone for its disastrous toll on the souls of men. Nothing short of a powerful spiritual movement, strong enough to renovate a decaying civilization, can halt the modern slide to moral suicide. The 1904 revival did just that because it was of God. Today the remedy still lies with Him.

Throughout the lean years of declension in the churches which followed the 1914-18 war it was 'the children of the revival' who maintained the spiritual glow in the prayer and society meeting and Sunday School. The faithful remnant within each denomination consisted mainly of the rank and file of revival converts. Gomer M. Roberts' rhetorical questions about the revival's lasting fruit are most suggestive : "Who can give an account of the lasting blessings of the 1904-5 revival? Is it possible to tabulate a sum total of family bliss, peace of conscience, brotherly love, and holy conversation? What of the debts that were paid, and the enemies reconciled to one another? What of the drunkards who became sober, and the prodigals who were restored? Is there a balance that can weigh the burden of sins which was thrown at the foot of the cross?"[6] The answers are self-evident.

Apostolic character

In many ways the meetings partook of an apostolic character. The passages in 1 Corinthians which end with "Let all things be done decently and in order" (chapter 14) portray the 'domestic scene' of the worshipping community, as distinct from the more 'public image' of the church at work in evangelism typified by Paul's missionary activities. The former depicts the exercise of spiritual gifts by the entire congregation, regulated by principles such as orderliness and edification value. The latter represents a more formal presentation of the basic Christian message.

This reversion to New Testament order during the revival may not have been a conscious, premeditated attempt, but its affinity to early Christian practice is unmistakable. The absence of liturgical order or formality was based on two related ideas, the universality of spiritual gifts, and the priesthood of all believers.

Evan Roberts' methods

Evan Roberts looked upon the revival meetings as belonging to the 'domestic' activity of the church. "Bend the church and save the world" was his underlying conviction. His addresses were directed to that end, and whenever there were evidences of brokenness among the congregation he would often dispense with the address altogether. Evan Roberts' part in the revival is best defined as a ministry of gifts rather than a ministry of the Word.

Unhappily, Roberts did not always observe the biblical safeguards for the proper exercise of spiritual gifts. As a result, a ministry of the Word was often absent, depriving the congregations of basic teaching which was crucial not only to a right understanding of the faith, but also to ensure proper growth in it. This gave rise to some excesses of emotionalism, and placed the converts' experience at the mercy of individual idiosyncrasies and the psychological fashions of the day. The later repercussions were even more serious, for it led to a rapid decline in the spiritual discernment and vigour of many, whose love, unbuttressed by knowledge, grew sadly cold.

This is not to say that Roberts' ministry was totally without Scriptural or doctrinal content. The range of his subjects was wide, even though the treatment was not deep. His style was one of exhortation rather than exposition. In this way he spoke of God's infinity, of His greatness, and of the judgment day.[7] A recurring theme was Christ's love, but he also emphasized Christ's kingship.[8] The references to faith, repentance, forgiveness, and the elements of spiritual experience were especially prominent, but consistently related to the majesty and glory of God :

" 'O Iesu, plyg ni' (O Jesus, bend us), prayed a young man in the gallery, who said that, having seen Jesus, he could not now remain silent. He went on praying passionately, and when the singing of an English hymn had drowned the voice of the petitioner Mr. Evan Roberts declared that there was a want of liberty in the meeting, and he reminded them that 'perfect love casteth out fear'. The great need of our country and age was that of the greatness of God. He had sometimes noticed the creature commanding the Creator. The Church had a duty to perform in teaching, especially the young converts, the proper idea of the greatness of God. There was no need to shout to Him, for He was near—close to them. There had been, and were still, some light-hearted people in that congregation who must realize the greatness and the proximity of God. They needed clean hands and clean hearts."[9]

Throughout the early months of the revival he repeatedly proposed his four prerequisites to blessing, and crystallized these into the phrase "bend the church and save the world". His appeal was experimental rather than theological. It was in this respect more than any other that the Welsh revival of 1904 differed from previous visitations, and if this was its distinguishing feature, it was also its incipient danger.

Supremely, the subject of Roberts' sermons was 'revival'. Usually his address was brief and not based on any one text, the following being delivered at Blaen-cwm, a Rhondda village, on the 30th of November :

"God's three great gifts to the world are the Bible, His Son, and the Holy Spirit. Have you received them? We shall read the Bible in vain, if we do so on the Sabbath only . . . Once you behold Christ as your Saviour, you will be hungering and thirsting to read the Bible, and will surmount all the obstacles in the way . . . God's second gift is His beloved Son. Have you ever thought how difficult it was for Abraham to place Isaac, his son, on the altar? If you have, you can think of the feeling of the Father, giving His own Son. That is a feeling that cannot be described. If the Father has given Him, have you received Him? . . . Remember, He will not come to stubborn people. If you are disobedient, ask Him to bend you; not to save you now, but bend you . . . Sooner or later, you must be bent. Either grace or wrath must bend you. If the Church be on its knees, the world will be on its feet . . . Do all to glorify Him, and remember to do it, as He asks. I was on fire with a desire to go to arouse the Churches of Wales, but I was not allowed to go at once. I had to wait from three weeks to a month, in order to learn the great lesson of giving the glory to God. And as soon as I was able to say, 'May it all be to Thy glory', I was allowed to go . . . Now, we must have four things in order to get the Holy Spirit . . . 1. You must obtain full and complete pardon for the sins of the past . . . 2. Is there anything doubtful in your life? If so, it must be removed and done away with . . . If you shall have to ask the forgiveness of brothers and sisters, bend to the work at once . . . We must rid the churches of all bad feeling—all malice, envy, prejudice, and misunderstandings. Bow not in prayer until all offences have been forgiven : but if you feel you cannot forgive, bend to the dust, and ask for a forgiving spirit. You shall get it then. 3. Complete and immediate obedience to the Holy Spirit . . . 4. A public and personal confession of Christ . . ."[10]

While the revivalist's ideas were biblical, they were cast into an experimental mould, a mould determined by Roberts' own spiritual pilgrimage and designed for the express purpose of reviving the church.

The control of the Spirit

Nevertheless, it was not Roberts who determined either the progress or the success of the revival. The assessment of an eye-witness, W. T. Stead, confirms this : "Never was there a religious movement so little indebted to the guiding brain of its leaders. It seems to be going 'on its own'. There is no commanding human genius inspiring the advance". According to the same writer, the powerful manifestations emanated from no merely human source : "I found the flame of Welsh religious enthusiasm as smokeless as its coal. There are no advertisements, no brass bands, no posters, no huge tents. All the paraphernalia of the got-up job are conspicuous by their absence. Neither is there any organization, nor is there a director, at least none that is visible to the human eye".[11]

The periodicals of the day, religious and literary, drew attention to the various characteristics of the work. H. Elvet Lewis, writing to *The British Weekly,* mentioned two of these, "the unveiling of the cross, and the rediscovery of the power of intercessory prayer . . . The most effective hymns of the present Revival are in the key either of the sufferings of Jesus in the Garden or on Calvary, or of the gracious wonder of His atoning love . . . the prayer meeting is the generating station of all this powerful and far-spread current".[12] The Calvinistic Methodist monthly, *Y Drysorfa,* spoke of "the willingness of the people, *especially the young people, to take a leading part",*[13] while the Baptist *Seren Gomer* emphasised the prominence given to the work of the Holy Spirit in the revival.[14] Both the Wesleyan *Eurgrawn,* and the literary *Geninen* referred to the theme of personal assurance of salvation evidenced by the converts. The latter also noted the sanctifying effects of this in making restitution and the longing for a life of communion with God.[15] Pre-eminently, therefore, it was in the realm of the application of redemption and the believer's apprehension of it, that the revival moved.

This subjective and individual element was not without its objective *raison d'être.* J. Vyrnwy Morgan speaks of it when he regards the chief value of the revival as being "its attitude to Christ" : "Every convert set Him in the same incomparable place, and acknowledged to Him the same immeasurable debt. Forgiveness through Him, salvation through Him, strength to stand, suffer and to overcome through Him. The new life in the Spirit, all that they had ceased to be, and all that they hoped to be—they owed it to Him. This was the one clear, definite note of the Revival—the ascendancy that Christ exercised over the people".[16]

Evan Roberts discounted all attempts and tendencies to impute any effecting agency to his own person or activity : the glory for the power belonged to God the Holy Spirit, and to Him alone. In this respect, the revivalist's conversation with W. T. Stead is conclusive : "When I talked with him, he said : 'The movement is not of me, it is of God. I would not dare to try to direct it. Obey the Spirit, that is our word in everything. It is the Spirit alone which is leading us in our meetings and in all that is done'.

" 'You do not preach or teach, or control the meetings?'

" 'Why should I teach when the Spirit is teaching? What need have these people to be told that they are sinners? What they need is salvation. Do they not know it? It is not knowledge that they lack, but decision—action. And why should I control the meetings? The meetings control themselves, or rather the Spirit that is in them controls them'."[17]

Others, too, recognized the control and power of the Holy Spirit. Hugh Jones, the Wesleyan missioner widely used at that time, wrote of the self-effacing zeal of the human instruments so that the Holy Spirit might have the sole prominence. He added that, to bring conviction and awakening, the Spirit used the truths faithfully preached and taught through the means of grace in previous years.[18]

The claims of the Keswick Movement

Both R. B. Jones and Jessie Penn-Lewis claimed that 'the hidden springs' and secret 'origins' of the 1904 revival were to be found in Keswick. In his book on the revival, *Rent Heavens,* Jones spoke of the Convention's "vital connection with the revival" in these words : "Keswick had not a little to do with the birth of the Revival, and many have wondered how it happened that, when it was born, the nurse did not seem to welcome as heartily as might be expected what was in large measure her child".[19] Jessie Penn-Lewis's book on the same subject, *The Awakening in Wales 1904-5,* pursues the same theme, and many have followed since.

At the time of the revival a similar claim was made by F.

B. Meyer from his own pulpit. On Sunday, 11th December, 1904, he asserted his instrumentality in bringing about the widespread blessings being experienced at that time in Wales, and his remarks were duly reported in the national press.

"The Rev. F. B. Meyer . . . surprised his congregation on Sunday morning (says the *Morning Leader*) by explaining that he was instrumental in giving birth to the greatest revival that has taken place in Wales for over half a century. The rev. gentleman said that in August of last year, while preaching at a Convention in Wales, he stopped in the middle of his sermon to ask whether his audience should not 'here and now' magnify their Lord. The entire congregation instantly sprang to their feet and sang with the wildest enthusiasm, 'Crown Him, Crown Him!' That was the beginning. At the close of the service five or six young ministers came to Mr. Meyer and said, 'We'll spend a whole day once a month until you come again praying for a revival'. They did, and Mr. Evan Roberts, a young miner, who heard Mr. Meyer's powerful address, attended the monthly whole-day prayer meetings, while in his spare time he studied theology under a tutor."[20]

Nearly thirty years of Keswick Convention ministry had not 'given birth' to revival in England. Wales on the other hand, as has been shown, had been repeatedly blessed throughout the nineteenth century, including the period of Keswick's freshest impact, and yet quite independently of it. Welshmen immediately associated the spiritual manifestations of those days with God's past revival activity in their land, and Meyer's establishing himself as the founder of a Welsh revival 'movement' was to them incomprehensible.

It is understandable therefore that a Welsh spokesman's repudiation of Meyer's claim should have been violent. Cynddylan Jones wrote to the *Western Mail* of 22nd December :

"The Rev. Mr. Meyer and others advance their claims to be the originators of the Welsh Revival. The publication of the former's claim created a painful impression. After an interview with Mr. Evan Roberts I wish to say to these claimants for honour : 'Silence ! Silence in the presence of the Lord !' This is the Lord's doing, not yours, directly or indirectly, and it is marvellous in our eyes. Mr. Meyer is only a shadowy name to the young revivalist, who has never seen nor heard him. For thirteen years God has been training this young Welshman."

Clearly, it was misleading and erroneous to refer to the revival as the child of Keswick, for Evan Roberts' spiritual lineage lay in the direction of a deep-rooted Welsh Calvinistic Methodist tradition rather than in a novel English holiness movement.

An indication of this is the type of hymn which was so widely sung during the revival. The fact that they were Welsh hymns may have contributed to the geographical limits of the revival, but they gave expression to the truths of redemption and assurance rather than holiness and consecration. They were drawn from the eighteenth century evangelical revival rather than from the nineteenth century Keswick *Hymns of Consecration and Faith*. To the Welsh churches in 1904-05 the revival had affinities with the mighty acts of God going back to the time of Daniel Rowland and Howel Harris, John Elias and David Morgan. Any attempt to define it in terms of a large-scale holiness movement would have been artificial and unconvincing. Cynddylan Jones, writing at such close proximity to the events, could even then foresee this very danger, and spoke of it in the same article :

"Is the revival likely to continue? Yes, till it has done its work . . . We do not want it to last longer—the tension is too great . . . Will it extend? Through Wales, yes; through England, doubtful. However, it depends upon England itself. Given the necessary conditions, the Spirit will descend. The Saxon race works by mechanics, the Celts by dynamics—that makes all the difference in the world. And here precisely lies the danger of the present movement. Wales has never had professional missioners—we have no equivalent word in our language, because the thing is alien to our nature and habits. Here is the peril : that Evan Roberts will fall into the hands of the religious showmen, who are always on the look-out for new lions . . . The other danger is that the professional missioners will try to capture the movement. They are already gathered like eagles ready for their prey. To all these I say, in the name of Wales : Hands off ! Come and see and get the blessing; return home, and pass the blessing on. 'I want to learn the secret', said one of these missioners to Mr. Evan Roberts, as though there was a trick or secret spring to be touched by the operator. 'I have no secret', replied the young preacher, 'ask and ye shall receive'."

It is hard to avoid the impression that Cynddylan Jones' fears were realized in spite of this prophetic warning. The Welsh contingent of three hundred at the Keswick Convention of 1905 proved an embarrassment to the leaders. As J. C. Pollock notes in his authorized history *The Keswick Story*, to Evan Hopkins and others "the cries and songs had a professional touch : the Welsh, not the Holy Spirit, were turning Keswick revivalist". Even more baffling to the Keswick authorities was Evan Roberts himself. It seems strange, in the light of the Keswick attempts to foster the revival, that he was not asked to give several addresses at the Convention on the subject, even though they would not have woven easily into the rigid Keswick pattern.

An invitation was however extended to him to give a special address when he attended the Convention in 1906, but according to Pollock "he merely sat silent on the platform, and stood and prayed silent. The meeting developed into a rather hysterical prayer meeting with people praying simultaneously all over the tent and was finally made to conclude by the chairman." In this context Pollock's comment is interesting : "England did not blaze. Whether the Keswick Convention had misinterpreted its role is an imponderable of history : there may be significance in that Keswick continued service to the church while Evan Roberts suffered nervous breakdown and retired from the public eye for the remainder of his long life."[21] Apart from the fact that this statement requires modification (see chapter 11) Evan Roberts's relationship to Keswick and its supporters—notably F. B. Meyer and Jessie Penn-Lewis—came to the attention of the Welsh public again in 1909.

An anonymous article in the *South Wales Daily News* of July 10th reported that Evan Roberts had refused not only offers by the Free Church Council to become a missioner, but also ordination by the Calvinistic Methodist Church. The reason alleged was the influence of Jessie Penn-Lewis, with whom he had been staying since the revival, in favour of his enlistment as missioner under the Keswick banner. Two days later the following disavowal from the revivalist himself appeared in the same newspaper :

"No overtures have been made to me by the National Free Church Council . . . I have no recollection of any offer of ordination, officially made to me by the Calvinistic body . . . since my breakdown in health the subject has not been mentioned to me . . . I have not relinquished either intention or desire to return to Wales for mission work, although it is certainly beyond my power to 'inaugurate a fresh revival', for revival can alone be given by the Holy Spirit of God when the conditions are fulfilled. I am not equipping myself for mission work under the auspices of any 'movement'. I have not yet come to any decision concerning my future work. I am desired by Mrs. Penn-Lewis to say (as I am now writing to you) that the statements made by the writer of the article concerning her 'views' are incorrect and have no foundation in fact."

In spite of the fact that Mrs. Penn-Lewis discounted the rumour in this second-hand way, there seems to be some evidence of collusion on the part of the Penn-Lewises and F. B. Meyer, in order to restrict influences other than those sanctioned by themselves from reaching the revivalist.

Alien influences

An example of this is provided by a correspondence which forms an Appendix to J. Vyrnwy Morgan's verbose and short-sighted book *The Welsh Religious Revival* which was published in the same year. On hearing of its intended publication F. B. Meyer wrote to the author expressing concern "that nothing of adverse criticism of the past may affect either him (Evan Roberts) or the work of God through him". Morgan replied with details of the proposed study assuring him on the matter and inviting a written contribution. Meyer, however, was leaving for Turkey in a matter of days and informed Morgan, "the only thing I can do is to send your very kind letter to Mrs. Penn-Lewis, asking her to send any information which you ought to be in possession of". No explanation was offered as to why it was being forwarded to her rather than to the revivalist himself. Naturally, Morgan was dissatisfied and would not accept any representations from either of these correspondents. "I could not, and would not change or modify my position on the points in question unless the statements or corrections came to me direct from Mr. Evan Roberts himself." Mrs. Penn-Lewis was "disappointed" at this attitude, and acknowledged that the revivalist had not been shown her letter to Morgan claiming to know Roberts's mind on the relevant subjects. Morgan was incensed and sent a severe reprimand : "You took a daring responsibility in approaching me in the way you did, and on a matter of such importance. If Mr. Evan Roberts had 'suffered', it is through those who constituted themselves his bodyguard and advisers, claiming to speak in his name. They have sought to surround his personality with clouds of marvel, miracle and sacredness, which has done much towards marring his usefulness." The correspondence closed with an apology from Mrs. Penn-Lewis.

This reluctance to allow Roberts unhindered converse with the outside world may have been due to legitimate motives, such as concern over his physical health, but it could not fail to create an impression of secrecy, suspicion, and mistrust. With the appearance, three years later, of *War on the Saints* written by Jessie Penn-Lewis "in collaboration with Evan Roberts", and in the light of her withdrawal from Keswick circles, it seemed as if the revivalist had been commandeered for Jessie Penn-Lewis's private deployment. At any rate, during those years immediately after the revival, she was the only one who had free access to him. Any projected return by the revivalist to his native land for active ministry floundered on the rocks of this unhappy withdrawal and he was lost to Wales for a number of years. A connection, however, was maintained between Keswick and the young converts of the revival by means of convention ministries, especially those of Llandrindod and Ammanford.

The prominence of women

Other women besides Mrs. Penn-Lewis were prominent in the revival period, including Rosina Davies and Florrie Evans in Wales, and Pandita Ramabai and Amy Carmichael in India. Participation by women in the work of the churches had been the subject of discussion at the Llandudno Association of the Calvinistic Methodists in November 1897. The sending of women missionaries to foreign lands had been accepted practice for a number of years, but the needs of the Home Mission and the Forward Movement brought the issue of the ministry of women into the open.

The Association's minutes urged the need for "our younger sisters" in such secular vocations as nursing and the hospital services. They also recorded : "We consider that the time has arrived when we . . . should make some arrangement for securing the services of some of these sisters, who are prepared to offer themselves for the work of the Saviour's kingdom in our midst.' The matter seems to have been discussed on the level of expediency rather than of biblical principle.

During the latter half of the nineteenth century women were taking an increasingly prominent part in philanthropic enterprises. The list of distinguished contributors to the field of social welfare (from evangelical principles and often for evangelistic purposes) is a long one: Elise Sandes and Mrs. Daniell for soldiers, Mrs. Smyly and Annie Macpherson for children, Catherine Marsh for temperance, Mrs. Susannah Meredith for prisoners, to name only a few.[22] Local Government Acts in 1888 and 1893 legislated for limited women's suffrage in certain areas of social administration, and these were significant precursors of the Suffragette Movement.

The teaching of Scripture, however, establishes clearly defined limits to the public ministry of women in the life of the church. On the one hand, the dignity of womanhood and family life is firmly established by Christ's attitude, apostolic instruction, and the practice of the New Testament church.[23] On the other hand, a public exercise of ministerial and teaching duties is expressly forbidden.[24]

The reason for this goes back to God's created order whereby the woman's nature is such as to follow rather than to lead. Her spiritual equality with man as a recipient of God's grace is unquestioned,[25] but for the purpose of public worship the woman is not constitutionally equipped by God for a teaching rôle. Her part is one of submission rather than authority.[26]

At the time of the revival this Scriptural norm was not always observed. Its omission left the movement open to emotional excesses and to a related failure in providing adequate doctrinal foundations.

Comparison with the 1859 Revival

These factors pin-point some of the differences between the Welsh revivals of 1859 and 1904. The former had faced opposition in its early phases, the 1904 in its later. Publicity in the national press secured for the 1904 revival widespread and rapid acceptance, while in 1859 progress was slower. In keeping with so many previous Welsh revivals, that of 1859 had been of a theological and doctrinal nature. The 1904 work gave greater prominence to human emotion expressed in prayer, testimony and song. This was, doubtless, in accordance with the theological fashions of the respective generations, but the 1904 characteristics were not conducive to the solid establishment of either Christian conviction or character.

Greater care was taken during 1859 in assessing Christian experience than in 1904. The criteria of accepting as valid any profession of faith were, in the latter, less stringent, more superficial, and almost entirely subjective. Little cognizance was taken of a person's understanding and knowledge of the Christian faith, his reasons for a Christian hope, or his discernment between truth and error. Far more importance was attached to experimental considerations of conviction and confession of sin, of the traumatic experience of conversion, of the joy of forgiveness and the assurance of salvation. Few saw the need for a Scriptural foundation to estimate their original authenticity, persevering quality, and progressive value.

A great deal of the blame for this serious deficiency must be attributed to the neglect of a biblically-based and doctrinally sound preaching ministry. The greatest need of that hour of God's visitation in the land had been the exercise of the God-ordained agency of preaching the Word of God.

The seeds of a future declension were, sadly, sown at a time of revival. The harvest yet to be reaped, of a declining membership and empty churches, of a secular society and an adulterated gospel, was to be bitter indeed.

The supremacy of the Word of God in every work of God is a divinely ordained principle. It applies with greater relevance and importance than ever to a gracious season of revival.

CHAPTER 11

MILITANT AFTERMATH

BY the autumn of 1905 Roberts' influence had waned. He was still sought after by many, but his revival activities dwindled. In October his soul was agitated and restless :

"It is a mistake for me to try and arrange and carry out my future. The people cannot understand why I do not move; and I fail to understand why I am staying! But this I know, that I am moving swifter than ever—so swift, indeed, that I cannot perceive myself moving. What a commotion there is in the tents! My soul is a kind of tabernacle, and self dwelling in innumerable tents around it, and what takes place is the slaughtering of the troublesome, howling, thankless, rebellious inhabitants, and so on. Oh! some ceaseless moving continues! The old man and the pure heart enraging, and getting furious for victory."[1]

His spasmodic, erratic, and disjointed attempts at holding revival meetings in South and North Wales during the following months only tired his body. At the end of January 1906 he confessed to being "quite run down at the end of the Caernarvonshire mission", and that he would "take it slowly now".[2] A visit to Gloucester in March included the cathedral, and he was shown the memorials to George Whitefield, Robert Raikes, and Bishop John Hooper. Opposite his signature in the visitors' book he wrote, "My God, give me the bishop's disposition".[3]

A month later Evan Roberts had retired "for a time of rest and recuperation" to the home of Mr. and Mrs. Penn-

Lewis near Leicester. Of this period Mrs. Penn-Lewis' biographer wrote :

"His recovery, however, was slow and intermittent, lasting many months, and during the long period of convalescence, he began to open his mind to his hostess on many experiences of supernatural forces witnessed during the Revival. Since her own mighty enduement of power for service, Mrs. Penn-Lewis had learned the path of the Cross, and seen the dangers attendant upon souls who, having experienced such a breaking-through into the supernatural realm, do not know *identification with Christ in His death* as the place of safety from the wiles and assaults of the devil . . . This God-given knowledge and experience, together with the insight into the devices of the enemy gained by Mr. Roberts in his experiences during the Revival, are conserved to the Church of God in *War on the Saints*."[4]

His presence at a convention "for the deepening of the spiritual life" in Bangor in the middle of April passed almost unnoticed, the main speakers being E. Keri Evans and W. W. Lewis.[5]

Writing from Leicester in May he reflected Jessie Penn-Lewis' characteristic teaching : "How does the work of the Cross go on? . . . There is nothing like the Cross of our Lord to melt the hardest hearts. It is the wisdom and power of God in the uplifting of mankind. But are we, its followers, loyal to Him who endured it? The Cross is the Throne . . . Is the Cross in its power to remove 'sins' and 'self' eagerly accepted by the people today?"[6]

In June he accompanied Mrs. Penn-Lewis to meetings at Porth, and in July to the Keswick convention.[7] Her book *The Warfare with Satan and the Way of Victory* appeared about that time, and its theme of the Christian's spiritual conflict with evil spirits was to find fuller expression in *War on the Saints* which was published six years later. They worked together for a number of years, Roberts confining his public ministry to occasional prayer conferences in England.[8]

From 1907 he gave himself almost exclusively to a ministry of intercessory prayer. Denying a rumour that he was to conduct a religious campaign in Anglesey in October 1932, he said :

"My work is confined to prayer, and it is to such that I have devoted myself for the last 25 years . . . There are just two things . . . prayer and preaching—mine is locked up in the first. I work as hard at prayer as if I had undertaken any other form of religious work . . . By preaching I would reach the limited few—by and through prayer I can reach the whole of mankind through God. But I am afraid that people do not understand what all this means and what it involves".[9]

He maintained an interest in the affairs of the Calvinistic Methodists, and in 1910 a telegram of good wishes from Roberts to its General Assembly was cordially received and reciprocated. The denomination that year resolved "to organise a great Evangelistic Campaign throughout the churches", and in the telegram to Roberts the hope was expressed that he would soon return to Wales to help in the work of evangelism.[10]

Roberts' later ministry

He paid a brief visit to see his sick father in January 1927, and a year later spent a week-end in London with Samuel Jenkins, one of the singers of the revival.[11] The same year witnessed a return to his native village, occasioned by the funeral of his father and also by the importunity of a prayer group under the leadership of Miss Mary Davies of the Post Office, Gorseinon. His extended visit enabled him to take part in the services held to commemorate the centenary of Moriah. To the large congregation which had gathered in the knowledge of his attendance he appeared "calm", "fervent, yet restrained".[12]

It was at the prayer meetings of the group led by Mary Davies, however, that the powerful impressions of the revival were renewed. The group had come into existence in November 1928, and had increased in number to about thirty. With evidences of the Holy Spirit working in their midst the group sent for Roberts, and their meetings continued for several months. Many people were converted as a result of prayers offered on their behalf in the group meetings, and the numbers attending them increased to about sixty.

In their midst Evan Roberts exercised to the full his ministry of spiritual gifts. The sick were anointed and healed, and evil spirits were exorcised. While Roberts continued his emphasis on being filled with the Holy Spirit, he did not practise the laying on of hands for that purpose. On more than one occasion he prophesied future events, and since 1914 had adopted a pre-millennial view of the second coming of Christ. Throughout this period his ministry was characterised by a vivid awareness of the spiritual conflict with Satan and evil spirits.

Nearby Pontardulais was visited by him in February 1930, and four months later he took part in the public meetings of the Calvinistic Methodists' General Assembly.[13] He spoke at the Forward Movement and children's meetings, took the devotional exercises at the Communion Service, and participated in the "seiat" on "The power of the Holy Spirit".[14] From Mold he proceeded to the Ammanford convention where he led the morning prayer meetings, and at a revival commemoration service emphasised "the lasting effect of the revival upon the religious life of Wales".[15]   Later that month he visited Llangeitho in Cardiganshire, the scene of many eighteenth century revivals, and St. David's cathedral.[16]

In August he attended meetings connected with the National Eisteddfod.   At a Welsh Societies' reunion in Llanelli he said that, "having been called of God to deliver a message to Wales and to the world, he had since been in exile for very many years.   God sent him into exile to pray for the world, but during these years his native land was very much on his mind".[17]   The burden of his remarks at the Eisteddfod itself was the need for another revival.[18]   Speaking at Cardigan over a year later his theme was prophecy, but he also referred to his withdrawal to seclusion and exile : "At the end of the 1904 revival I was led by the Spirit and taken over the border into England, and I had the burden cast upon me.   I have not been idle.   I have been praying and watching the fulfilment of the prophecy."[19]   From 1930 until his death in 1951 he resided in Cardiff.[20]   To the end, his ministry remained a ministry of gifts rather than a ministry of the Word.   He was buried in Moriah cemetery, Loughor, and a memorial in his honour, situated at the front of the church, was unveiled in 1953.

Church discipline

The years following a revival have always been regarded as vital.   The quickening of spiritual life and activity in the Church inevitably raises the thorny question of disciplinary standards.   Laxity with regard to this New Testament practice leads to impurity, often unrecognized and seldom bemoaned. With its restoration at a time of revival there is a sharp rise in the incidence of church members disciplined for unworthy conduct. This does not mean that the revival was spurious, it merely indicates a reversion to apostolic order.

The historic denominations sometimes found difficulty in absorbing the spiritual harvest on account of their incapacity to provide the necessary environment of fellowship, discipline, and instruction. W. B. Sprague in his notable *Lectures on Revivals* summarized the Church's responsibility to the new converts as being three-fold; to save from self-deception, to build up in faith, and in holiness. Ideally, therefore, the resources and agencies of the Church should be directed towards maintaining her purity, stability, efficacy, and unity.

Admission into nonconformist church membership at the turn of the present century was still preceded by a period of probation. The Calvinistic Methodists had laid down well-defined criteria of discipline, their chief features being spiritual understanding, experience and resolution, accompanied by moral and social uprightness. With the influx of such vast numbers it is understandable that these were not always strictly observed.

Lack of solid preaching

The able and conscientious Congregationalist minister, E. Keri Evans, admitted that the love of many grew cold and that the progress of others was erratic through dependence on an occasional shower of blessing rather than on the steady, sanctifying influences of the Holy Spirit.[21] It can hardly be questioned that this unsteady development in the Christian life of the converts would have been eliminated had there been an insistence upon preaching at the time of the revival. There is no substitute for the sustained and comprehensive presentation of God's truth, for Christ rules His Church by His Word and Spirit.

Inevitably, therefore, there was a falling away among the

converts of the revival. This was reckoned to be about 20 per cent altogether over the five or six years which followed. Referring to their stability in 1907, H. Elvet Lewis felt that "those who were brought in with the morning dew of the revival, at the home-born prayer meetings, stand better than those who came later, with the excitement and heat of mixed and crowded audiences. While the simple but irresistible power of prayer was honoured and trusted, the work of grace proved most effectual and most lasting."[22]

Nevertheless, there was during the revival a culpable neglect of the divinely-ordained instrument of preaching. Evan Roberts, it is true, looked on prayer as a converting ordinance, and his public exposition of Scripture was accordingly curtailed to allow for more prayer. This practice presumed on the preaching of the past, and a writer on the work in India acknowledged such indebtedness : "This Revival has made it very evident that our imperfect labour in teaching the Christians in years gone by has not been in vain; they could never have uttered the heartfelt, thoughtful, Scriptural prayers we often heard but for the Bible teaching they have received."[23] If it proved an encouraging tribute to the past it could not, and did not, provide a sufficient foundation for the future.

Regrettably, the organised attempts to provide solid instruction for the new converts hardly proved adequate. This was partly due to a lack of suitable leadership. There was no organizing genius of the calibre of Howel Harris to "settle" and regulate "little fellowship meetings" for the converts. Neither was there a Daniel Rowland to ensure a full-orbed presentation of the gospel. It was also due to the intrinsic weaknesses of the means which were in fact provided at the time. The Ammanford convention was more than a decade away in the future, and its ministry would be geographically limited.

Damaging influences

Nearer the- time a Welsh book specially written for the converts of the revival served to channel their thinking on purely Keswick principles, and limited their view of the Christian life to the horizons of cleansing, consecration, abiding in Christ, and the fulness of the Spirit.[24] This was fundamentally misleading, and it deprived the converts of that humbling, awe-inspiring vision of the whole counsel of God which was at once their spiritual heritage and their greatest need. By 1905 the Llandrindod convention had already been established as an outpost of the English holiness movement. It did not cater for the Celtic temperament and left the Welsh spiritual tradition tragically impoverished. In this respect the revival failed to recognize its own nationalism. Consequently, it also failed to provide a distinctively indigenous and thoroughly sympathetic teaching ministry.

There were other, still more tragic, factors. The rise of the new theology and the emergence of psychological categories for the interpretation of religious experience have already been noted. The former deprived the revival of a stable doctrinal foundation, the latter imposed on it false standards of reference. Failure to recognise the presence of these damaging influences led to erroneous appraisal of the revival's achievements. Thus R. Tudur Jones' recent assessment is deficient at this very point: "There is something lamentable rather than creative about this revival . . . no sooner was the revival over than people's interests turned to politics, to the new theology, to social struggles . . ."[25] It has already been shown that the interest of the churches had been this way inclined for at least a decade before the revival. The

interest of the converts lay in the direction of more conservative theology and more spiritual pursuits. As a result, when
this conflict of allegiance and affinities became apparent, many
of them felt that the only remedy was ecclesiastical separation.

The figure of twenty per cent did not represent a solid
defection back into the world. On the contrary, by far the
greater part of this figure represented a defection not *from*
Christianity but *within* it. This is a point which has been
totally ignored by commentators on the revival. The newly-
emergent left-wing denominations, the separated mission halls
and the Pentecostal-Apostolic churches, have been either
slanderously misrepresented as perversions, or else they have
been dishonestly written off as irrelevant. A recognition of
their sustained contribution to twentieth century Christianity
would demolish the idea of the revival being a lamentable fact
rather than a creative force.

The question of disestablishment

When the forces at work in the revival waned, there was
a ready-made burning religious and political issue to be
resolved. This was the battle over the disestablishment of
the Welsh Anglican church, which had been looming larger
in the years preceding the revival and had merely been shelved
during it. Ecclesiastically speaking, Welsh Anglicanism as an
establishment had been an anachronism for several decades.
Its continuance into the twentieth century was entirely due
to an ecclesiastical version of English colonialism, witness the
fact that a motion for disestablishment in the Parliament of
1886 was lost, even though twenty-eight of the thirty-four
Welsh members voted for it.[26] The decline of its influence
was due partly to an individualism in the Celtic temperament,
and partly to an inflexibly English cultural ethos in the
Establishment.

In the matter of the Welsh language, for instance, influence was brought to bear on some clergymen to teach English as a means of getting the parishioners to participate fully in the English liturgy. There were those, like Griffith Arthur Jones, vicar of a rural Merionethshire parish, who vigorously opposed such alien insinuations : "I am not a teacher of languages, but a priest of God's Church, and my duty is to teach the people religion in the language they understand."[27] Nevertheless, the fundamental orientation of Welsh Anglicanism lay in the direction of Canterbury rather than Cardiff or Caernarvon.

The rôle of the 1904 revival in effecting disestablishment was certainly not pivotal. It merely served to consolidate the nonconformist majority in the same way as previous revivals had done. Perhaps it was providential rather than significant that the revival broke out a mere one year before the return of a sympathetic Liberal government, a mere two years before the Royal Commission on the issue, and a mere decade before the bill finally became law.

Doctrinal conflict

The influence of the 1904 revival was more important in the constitutional history of the Calvinistic Methodists. In the 1920s there was a great deal of discussion within the denomination about its Confession of Faith. The Constitutional Deed of 1826 had been framed to ensure strict adherence to the denomination's doctrinal tenets, and to provide a corresponding legal safeguard for its places of worship. By 1912 there had been an attempt in the courts of the church to secure the framing of a "Shorter Declaration of Faith", an oblique and indirect criticism of both content and length of the confession being implied.[28] Later, the reports of the Reconstruction Commission, which had appeared in the early twenties, strongly urged parliamentary legislation to modify these requirements.

Nantlais Williams, one of the revival's most illustrious converts, was in the vanguard of the opposition to this move. His objections were grounded on the conviction that the advocates of a liberal theology were seeking the legal and doctrinal leverage necessary both to take over the denominational machinery and to bring about a radical change in the evangelical nature of its witness.

He maintained that the liberals were agitating for reform purely as a matter of political manoeuvre. It was a deceptive strategy on their part to gain power in the courts of the church. They were ecclesiastical cuckoos seeking to gain fraudulent control of the evangelical nest. Unable to set up their own churches through the impotence of their modernist message, they sought to supplant the churches of the Methodist Fathers, established by evangelical zeal for the "old" gospel.

Their cry for "freedom" sounded laudable until Williams observed : "We are not bound by the law, so much as by the Fathers and their scriptural, evangelical faith". He exposed the doctrinal dishonesty and moral indifference of their position, for the modernist faith "did not have enough confidence in itself to venture forth to raise a temple to disseminate it. It must rather endeavour to usurp the right to those buildings put up at the expense of the Confession of Faith . . . It will be robbing what rightly belongs to others."[29]

In the discussion which followed through the columns of the denomination's weekly he further charged the modernists with double-talk, a device which utterly confused the common people. The scriptural and historical content of the most fundamental concepts were being shamelessly debased. There could be no prosperity to the church which thus betrayed the truth. A devaluation of the Christian currency could only lead to disaster. Nor would the ecumenical aspirations which motivated the leaders of the reconstruction movement be best served in an atmosphere of doctrinal fog. The interests of both sides could only benefit by clarity, honesty, and charity.

Later, Williams acknowledged that "it was something received in 1904 which encouraged me to stand so resolutely throughout the debate".[30] The issue was finally resolved when note was taken of his insistence on the inclusion in the Declaratory Statement of clear affirmations regarding the Deity of Christ, His virgin birth, His atoning death, His literal resurrection on the third day, and His second coming. The draft document was modified accordingly, and the 1933 Act of Parliament which remains the law of the church incorporates these determinative truths. In this way the 1904 revival has left an abiding mark on the legal structure of that ecclesiastical body.

In spite of these brave efforts it was a hollow victory for orthodoxy. One result of the reconstruction movement was the drawing up of the long-awaited "Shorter Declaration of Faith". In its wake T. Nefyn Williams, a minister who had been disciplined for heterodox views in 1928, was able to seek, and receive, readmission with a clear conscience. In his pamphlet *Y Ffordd yr Edrychaf ar Bethau* (The Way I Look at Things), as the title suggests, he rejects biblical and confessional authority in favour of his own moral consciousness. This subjectivist criterion led him to deny all supernatural elements in the gospel narrative from the virgin birth to the bodily resurrection of Christ. It followed that he ridiculed the biblical concepts of original sin and substitutionary atonement. While his expulsion in 1928 had been an unavoidable necessity, his restoration in the 1930s—without repentance or retraction —marked the beginning of an epoch.

From being an honest dissenter he became the champion of doctrinal deviationists. They used the "Shorter Declaration of Faith" to salve their conscience from the demands of the fuller and more explicit confession. If the age of doctrinal confusion had not dawned, when men would use theological terms evacuated of their full traditional and biblical meaning, it was enough to take shelter under an all-embracing theological umbrella of general concepts. It was an era of dwindling doctrinal requirements. The disintegration of orthodoxy had become an accomplished fact within at least one of the historic denominations.

The baptism of the Holy Spirit

In contrast with this pathological tendency one of the main issues of the revival's aftermath concerned the rise of a vigorous Pentecostalism. The main reason for it was the prominence given to Pentecostal manifestations during the revival. Evan Roberts himself was chiefly responsible for this emphasis, not only on account of his experiences, but also by means of his public teaching. He had experienced the direct power of the Holy Spirit at home each night for a sustained period of time, and with agonizing intensity at Blaenannerch. It is strange that in the public mind, and to some extent in his own, Roberts' experience at Blaenannerch eclipsed that at Loughor in the Spring of 1904. True, the former was nearer in time to the breaking out of the revival, but it was not greater in importance. Although the Blaenannerch experience was more fierce in its intensity, it was of shorter duration than that which preceded it in chronological order. The first was private and sustained over a period of months; the second was public and limited to one particular occurrence.

Evan Roberts classified these experiences as "the baptism of the Holy Spirit". Such had been his prayer before that

remarkable night in Loughor. Later, his exposition of the
matter appeared in his joint work with Mrs. Penn-Lewis,
War on the Saints. Here they taught that this baptism is a
necessary prerequisite of revival : "The baptism of the Holy
Spirit is the essence of revival, for revival comes from a
knowledge of the Holy Spirit, and the way of co-working with
Him which enables Him to work in revival power. The
primary condition for revival is therefore, that believers should
individually know the baptism of the Holy Ghost." A full
definition of the term follows. "The baptism of the Holy
Spirit may be described as an influx, sudden or gradual, of the
Spirit of God into a man's spirit, which liberates it from the
vessel of the soul, and raises it into a place of dominance over
soul and body. The freed spirit then becomes an open channel
for the Spirit of God to pour through it an outflow of divine
power. The mind receives, at the same time, a clarifying
quickening, and the 'eye of the understanding' is filled with
light (Ephesians 1 :18). The body becomes entirely under the
man's complete control, as the result of the dominance of the
spirit, and often receives a quickening in strength for endur-
ance in the warfare service he finds he has emerged into."
Such "infilling of the Spirit" is stated explicitly to have been
"the cause of not only the revival in Wales in 1904-5, but of all
other revivals in the history of the world".[31]

The reference to a liberation of the spirit from the soul is
elsewhere in the book explained in terms of Hebrews 4 :12,
"For the word of God is quick, and powerful, and sharper than
any two edged sword, piercing even to the dividing asunder of
soul and spirit."[32] By virtue of this the carnal Christian
becomes spiritual, and his witness is more powerful. He is
released to serve God in a higher degree of holiness and
missionary usefulness. This is not to say that he is sinless. "Do
not think that you will be entirely rid of sin in this life even

after the baptism of the Spirit. Self will persist; you can never shake hands with self, and bid it good-bye."[33] On the other hand, "to be filled by the Spirit meant that they were being given greater strength and power".[34]

Roberts' ministry can only be fully understood in the light of this teaching. His revival activities and subsequent inter-cessory ministry are enigmatic unless due account is taken of the powerful and personal experiences at Loughor and Blaenannerch. To admit their reality and authenticity, if not their interpretation, is to allow Roberts a Spirit-enhanced awareness, discernment, and power which were at once the inspiration of his programme and the secret of his successs.

Pentecostalism

From the beginning, some of the leaders of an emerging Pentecostalism were interested in the revival, including Frank Bartleman and Joseph Smale in America, T. B. Barratt, of Norway, and Alexander Boddy, the vicar of Monkwearmouth near Sunderland.[35] While the movement's exponents in Wales drew their inspiration from the revival, their distinctly Pentecostal emphases were traceable to its rarer occurrences and incidental features. The mainstream of the revival con-tinued to run in the channels of the historic denominations without losing its impetus or character.

One of these exponents was George Jeffreys, the founder of the Elim Pentecostal Movement. Together with his brother, Stephen, he had been converted under the ministry of Glasnant Jones, a Congregationalist, in the time of the revival at their home in Nantyffyllon near Maesteg.[36] Having received the baptism of the Spirit, George Jeffreys sought opportunities to exercise a public ministry which would bear witness to this experience. Through the providential support of Cecil Polhill, one of the famous "Cambridge

Seven", he was able to receive Bible training under the auspices of the Pentecostal Missionary Union of Great Britain at its Preston Bible School. By 1914 Jeffreys had gained some prominence by reason of the success attending his campaigns in various parts of the British Isles. On the invitation of a group of Christians he crossed to Ireland where further converts were blessed with the Holy Spirit's baptism "with the Bible signs", including "speaking with new tongues". At his campaign centre, Monaghan, plans were drawn up for continuing this Pentecostal ministry in Belfast. With its establishment in 1915 the Elim Foursquare Gospel Alliance was founded.[87]

Apostolic Pentecostalism

Another Welshman of importance in the history of Pentecostalism was Daniel Powell Williams of Pen-y-groes in Carmarthenshire. He journeyed to Loughor on Christmas Day, 1904, where he came under severe conviction of sin and found release in Christ. Two years later he felt called to preach, but remained a miner. He first came into contact with the Pentecostal movement in 1909 while on holiday at Aberaeron on the Cardigan coast. He there

"Met a company of God's people who were baptized with the Holy Spirit. Daniel joined them and climbed a hill overlooking the bay. Here, as they were praising God, Daniel fell flat on his face, weeping, sobbing, and groaning, and he received the mighty baptism of the Holy Spirit. Ecstasy overwhelmed his soul, and he spoke with tongues as the Holy Spirit gave him utterance. As sure as Pentecost began a new era for the world so this Pentecost began a new era in the life of this lay preacher. He had studied for the ministry, but he still required the power of the Holy Spirit. Now he had received that power."[88]

He continued to preach in the churches, but inclined more and more to minister to those who believed in the baptism of the Spirit. In 1910 this latter group built an "evangelistic hall" in the village and Williams separated from the Congregationalists to join it.

Some time later he received "the Apostolic Vision", which led to his leaving the mine for full-time ministry, and separating from the "evangelistic hall" to be free to exercise his gift of "Apostolate". His call to "Apostleship" was formally received at a London convention in 1913. William Jones, his brother, had also been converted during the revival, but had backslidden. However, he was restored, and after his Spirit baptism emerged as a "prophet" in the Apostolic movement.

Apart from the baptism of the Holy Spirit, speaking in tongues is common in both Pentecostal and Apostolic churches. Daniel Williams records instances of these phenomena during the revival, and the sequel :

"The manifestation of the power was beyond human management. Men and women were mowed down by the axe of God like a forest. The glory was resting for over two years in some localities. Ministers could not minister, like Moses, when the cloud of glory came down on the Tabernacle. The weeping for mercy, the holy laughter, ecstasy of joy, the fire descending, burning its way to the hearts of men and women with sanctity and glory, were manifestations still cherished and longed for in greater power. Many were heard speaking in tongues and prophesying. So great was the visitation in Penygroes and the districts that nights were spent in the churches. Many witnessed to God's healing power in their bodies . . . Confusion and extravagance, undoubtedly, were present. But the Lord had His hand on His people, and they were preserved and were taught of God to persevere and pray,

and those that hankered and thirsted after God began to
assemble in cottages, seeking for the further manifestation of
His will. The news came of God's visitation in America.
Many came over to England. Sunderland became a centre
for many to receive the baptism, and the fire began to kindle
again. Gradually, the gifts were again manifested. The voice
of God was heard. The Apostolic Vision dawned, and some
had to face much misjudgment, but the purposes of God were
brought to birth in the days of adversity. The hand of the
Lord moved in a very strange way, and many of the brethren
in the Lord waxed confident, and became bold to declare the
revelation of God. The voice, with no uncertain sound to its
hearers, was opening new doors, and the Pentecostal flame ran
through the country, *and is still spreading*!"[39]

Its susceptibility to abuse led Evan Roberts to discourage
the exercise of the gift of tongues, "until the spiritual section
of the Church of Christ are more acquainted with the counter-
feiting methods of the spirit of evil, and the laws which give
them power of working, any testimony to such experience as
true, cannot be safely relied upon."[40]

As well as drawing upon the legacy of the holiness movement, Donald Gee points out that Pentecostalism was strongly
influenced and helped by the Welsh revival of 1904. "Its
most significant contribution was the creation of a widespread
spirit of expectation : 'Faith was rising to visualize a return to
apostolic Christianity in all its pristine beauty and power'."[41]
There can be no question that herein lay one of the revival's
most prominent characteristics, namely, its affinity to the spirit
of the New Testament worshipping community. Here were
all the ingredients : vivid experiences of the Holy Spirit's
power, free and spontaneous lay participation, agonizing conviction and holy joy. In the experience of some of the con-

verts, however, the ecstasy of the new wine was all too soon curbed by the frigidity of the old bottles.

The question of separation

The crusade for finding new bottles was not undertaken with enthusiasm or bitterness. While the majority of the converts remained within the historic denominations, for others separation became a necessity, not merely an expediency. "The dominant leaders in the earliest years of the Pentecostal Movement in the British Isles never encouraged the formation of separate Pentecostal assemblies as such . . . The counsel usually given was to 'receive the baptism in the Holy Spirit, but remain in your church, whatever the denomination may be'."[42] As early as 1911 T. B. Barratt was writing on the subject : "Pentecostal Centres are springing up in every country *outside the churches,* and in some lands will soon be found in every town and in every rural district. This is mainly due to the *opposition* the Revival has met from the churches generally. The same was the case *in Wales,* after the Revival there under Evan Roberts; the converts have extensively been obliged to band together and are called *'the children of the Revival',* the older Christian communities having in such cases *shut out* the fresh glorious flow of Revival grace and power, that God in his mercy sent them. *It is just so with this Pentecostal Revival*!"[43]

The totalitarian ecumenism of today cannot allow the possibility of defection within Christianity, only from it. This uncompromising imposition of uniformity within Christendom invalidates the ecumenist's claim to unity, and extinguishes the element of joyful freedom so evident in the New Testament churches' expression of worship. Christian unity and variety are not mutually exclusive.

A specific instance of expulsion from a historic denomination occurred at Cwmtwrch in the Swansea Valley in 1907, and crystallizes the issues facing non-Pentecostal separatists. The converts of the revival were given a thoroughly unacceptable ultimatum on a flimsy excuse and were compelled to withdraw in order to safeguard their testimony. It was this "testimony" of the assurance of salvation which proved in many cases objectionable to the traditionalists.[44] To perpetuate this testimony to the truths of regeneration by the Holy Spirit and redemption through the blood of Christ, these miners denied themselves many lawful commodities, with the result that a suitable place of worship was finished in 1912. They experienced tremendous blessing a year later under the ministry of Stephen Jeffreys, and still contribute substantially to the Christian witness in the area.

The 1904 revival was not the first to cause separation from existing denominations. The very creativity which Dr. R. Tudur Jones denies to the revival of 1904 he allows to the Welsh Congregationalists of the Puritan revival in the seventeenth century for their separating energy.[45] The separation of the Calvinistic Methodists from the Anglican church, marked by their first ordinations to the ministry in 1811, though delayed and overdue, was the direct result of the eighteenth century revival. In New England the same century witnessed powerful revivals with consequent, though less organized, defections within Christianity.

The unifying effect of revivals is often quoted by ecumenists in support of their programmes, but the subsequent persistence of denominational attitudes and the emergence of separating bodies is ignored. Historically speaking, it has to be admitted that revival has a divisive effect upon the Christian church. The best way to avoid division is to avoid revival. But to avoid revival is to allow the decaying process within the church to continue unabated to final extinction. For the church has no life in itself apart from the divine resuscitation.

The present situation

In an ecumenical age the validity of the concern to maintain the church's purity of truth and worship is denied, and its effect is stigmatized as sinful. Every effort is made to demolish the separating ideal and neutralize its existing witness. Coupled with an aversion to doctrinal orthodoxy, ecumenism displays a serious lapse in its historical awareness. Indeed, the instructive and humbling vista of church history seems to have invariably landed on the ecumenical blind-spot. An honest study of God's dealings in the past would have enabled the ecumenists to avoid making naïve pronouncements on "the sin of separation" in the church from the Protestant Reformation onwards.

The ecumenical ideal can only be realized by the propagation of the doctrine of an infallible church. This is why the Roman Catholic church can speak of its own unity; its doctrine of the exclusiveness and authority of the church safeguards it against separation from within its ranks. The triple doctrines restored at the Reformation of the sole authority of the Bible, the sole efficacy of grace, and the priesthood of all believers, not only restored direct access of the believer to God, but also restored diverse witness of the Church to men. In more ways than one it was the end of the Babylonish captivity of the Church, for it guaranteed not only the liberty of the Christian man, but also the liberty of the Christian Church. Thus the Protestant Reformation heralded in word and deed the ecclesiastical Magna Carta. It issued in clear, unmistakable terms a modern version of the divine charter of ecclesiastical freedom. The Church was no longer bound by the sombre grey colour of papist dogma and liturgy; she could now display in the full, multiple colours of the spectrum the whole counsel of God regarding His truth and His worship.

In this way the 1904 revival had a prismatic effect. The fresh light which broke forth from the New Testament was split up into a new variety of colours, not always acceptable to the old pattern. Its positive and beneficial contribution was the lead it gave to a re-examination of apostolic practice in the early church. There is no greater task facing the Church at the present time than a Scriptural assessment of its doctrinal purity, its functional government, and its missionary task.

Reformation is a prelude to revival. It is not possible to pray honestly for revival without first working diligently for reformation. The situation today, with its doctrinal confusion and ecumenical take-overs, demands renewed, uncompromising declaration of those divinely-revealed truths which have always been honoured in the great reforming movements of the ages. At the same time it must be remembered that no declaration, however convincing, can reproduce the powerful manifestations of the day of Pentecost, apart from the direct initiative of God the Holy Spirit.

Whatever may have been the aberrations introduced by human ingenuity subsequent to 1904, the revival in the period of its most powerful manifestations was unquestionably due to the divine initiative. In its origin there was so much of God's presence, in its extension so little of man's design; its effects were so evidently supernatural, its fruit so patently holy, that none could reasonably deny its divine source.

True revival always displays in unmistakable measure the ineffable glory of the divine attributes of omnipresence and omnipotence, of sovereignty and holiness, grace and righteousness. For several months of 1904 and 1905 much of Wales enjoyed this transforming vision. The gracious exhibition of the divine pity has invariably and indelibly marked such occasions as "times of refreshing from the presence of the Lord", instances of divine intervention in an otherwise impossible situation.

It has always been the Church's conviction that God's Word holds out the promise of such intervention in response to the cry of His children. For as God's truth is the ground of God's activity, so also God's promises are the hope of God's people.

LIST OF ABBREVIATIONS

CGD   Sidney Evans a Gomer M. Roberts (gol.), *Cyfrol Goffa Diwygiad 1904-1905*, 1954.

DD   *Y Diwygiad a'r Diwygwyr*, 1906.

DMPE   D. M. Phillips, Evan Roberts, *The Great Welsh Revivalist and his work*, Eighth edition, 1923.

DMPW   D. M. Phillips, *Evan Roberts a'i Waith*, Degfed argraffiad, 1924.

DWB   *Dictionary of Welsh Biography*.

JVM   J. Vyrnwy Morgan, *The Welsh Religious Revival 1904-5*, 1909.

NLW CMA   National Library of Wales, Calvinistic Methodist Archives.

RRW   'Awstin' and other special correspondents of the *Western Mail, The Religious Revival in Wales*, six pamphlets of collected newspaper reports issued in 1904-05.

WCAM   H. Elvet Lewis, *With Christ Among the Miners*, 1907.

REFERENCES

CHAPTER 1 REFERENCES

1. Eifion Evans, *When He Is Come*, Second Edition, 1967, p. 97.
2. The exact figures were 74 per cent. Nonconformist as compared to 26 per cent. Anglicans. See David Williams, *A History of Modern Wales*, 1951, pp. 266-7.
3. John Thomas, *Sunshine on the 'Hills' . . .*, Second Edition, 1875.
4. Edward Parry, *Llawlyfr ar Hanes y Diwygiadau Crefyddol yng Nghymru*, 1898, p. 157.
5. Alexander Sharp, *A Narrative of the Great Revival Work in South Wales*, 1871, c. 1872.
6. Edward Parry, *op. cit.*, pp. 160-1.
7. *ibid*, p. 162.
8. *ibid*, pp. 162-4.
9. *ibid*, pp. 164-5.
10. Henry Hughes, *Diwygiadau Crefyddol Cymru*, c. 1906, p. 458. For Richard Owen see DWB.
11. William Pritchard, *Cofiant y Parch. Richard Owen*, Third Edition, 1897, p. 21.
12. J. J. Morgan, *Dafydd Morgan a Diwygiad '59*, 1906, pp. 558-61.
13. *Y Drysorfa*, June, 1894; see also DWB.
14. William Pritchard, *op. cit.*, p. 140.

CHAPTER 2 REFERENCES

1. Howell Williams, *The Romance of the Forward Movement*, n.d., p. 37.
2. *ibid*, p. 53.
3. *O Gopa Bryn Nebo*, 1967, p. 71.
4. T. Mardy Rees, *Seth and Frank Joshua*, 1926, p. 114.
5. *ibid*, p. 57.
6. Edward Parry, *op. cit.*, 1898, pp. 157-8.
7. CGD, p. 85.
8. JVM, p. 124.
9. *Y Tyst*, October 12, 1904.
10. DD, p. 346.
11. WCAM, p. 44.
12. *Y Tyst*, October 5, 1904.
13. DD, pp. 133, 163.
14. *Yr Herald Cymraeg*, 14 March 1905, 'Y Diwygiad'.
15. Mary N. Garrard, *Mrs. Penn-Lewis, a Memoir*, Second Edition, c. 1947, p. 26.
16. *ibid*, p. 197.

17 *The Keswick Story*, 1964, p. 121.

18 Mary N. Garrard, *op. cit.*, p. 238.

19 For W. W. Lewis see *Y Goleuad*, June 1, 1938. Robert Ellis, *Living Echoes of the Welsh Revival*, includes among others chapters on W. W. Lewis, R. B. Jones and E. Keri Evans.

20 Robert Ellis, *op. cit.*, pp. 42-3.

21 *ibid*, p. 43.

22 *Rent Heavens*, pp. 30, 31.

CHAPTER 3 REFERENCES

1 W. Ambrose Bebb, *Yr Argyfwng*, 1954, pp. 30-3, 38. For Peter Price see JVM, pp. 141-162; and a series of articles in *Y Dysgedydd* commencing in August, 1953.

2 John A. T. Robinson, *Honest to God*, 1963, pp. 9-10.

3 *Theories of Revelation*, 1963, p. 30. McDonald goes on to say: "Demand was made by the English bishops, with the famous Thirlwall dissenting, that Colenso should be excommunicated. The result was a schism in the South African Church which was not eventually healed until nearly another half century had passed". cf. Iain Murray, *The Forgotten Spurgeon*, 1966, p. 147, quoting Spurgeon's sermon of 26th June, 1864, on Hebrews 13: 13.

4 H. D. McDonald, *op. cit.*, p. 28. cf. *Y Traethodydd*, July, 1945, pp. 120, ff, 'Y Dr. Lewis Edwards a Beirniadaeth Feiblaidd'.

5 H. D. McDonald, *op. cit.*, pp. 30-1; cf. Iain Murray, *op. cit.*, p. 147.

6 H. D. McDonald, *op. cit.*, pp. 33-6; cf. V. H. H. Green, *Religion at Oxford and Cambridge*, 1964, p. 316.

7 Quoted in Iain Murray, *op. cit.*, p. 149. The last four chapters of this book deal with the controversy.

8 pp. 504-5, 199.

9 See *Bathafarn*, xv, 7, an article by D. Llewelyn Jones, 'Drych o Ddechrau'r Ganrif', giving an extract from a periodical of 1899.

10 For David Adams see *Dictionary of Welsh Biography*, and R. Tudur Jones, *Hanes Annibynwyr Cymru*, 1966, pp. 249-50. See also William Evans, *An Outline of the History of Welsh Theology*, 1900, pp. 261-3.

11 H. Islwyn Davies, 'Y Dr. Lewis Edwards a Beirniadaeth Feiblaidd', *Y Traethodydd*.' July, 1945, p. 123. In his study of Edwards' life and work, Trebor Lloyd Evans assesses his contribution as giving intellectual content to a conservatively held orthodox position, and notes that "to be of the same mind as the Christian Church throughout the ages was more important to him than concurring with the sentiments of the latest authors" (*Lewis Edwards, Ei Fywyd a'i Waith*, 1967, p. 226).

12 J. Cynddylan Jones, *Athrylith a Gras* (1925), pp. 147-181, especi-

ally p. 158. On the basis of this address many approached the author to write a fuller treatment of the chief Christian beliefs, and this work appeared in four volumes under the title *Cysondeb y Ffydd* (The Concordance of the Faith, based on Romans 12 : 6) in 1905, 1907, 1912 and 1916.

13 *Y Goleuad*, April 4, 1900 (Cymanfa Ysgolion Sul Cyfarfod Misol Trefaldwyn Isaf).
14 *Y Goleuad*, March 7, 1900; *Y Drysorfa*, March, 1905, p. 105.
15 *Y Goleuad*, January 3, 1900 (Correspondence); *Y Goleuad*, January 17, 1900 (Correspondence).
16 *Yr Haul*, August 15, 1902.
17 *Y Goleuad*, April 11, 1900.
18 For Dean Howell see *Dictionary of Welsh Biography*. The same article appeared the following month (January, 1903) in *Y Dysgedydd*, pp. 17-19, under the title 'Prif Angen Cymru' (Wales' greatest need).
19 *Y Tyst*, October 19, 1904. According to H. Elvet Lewis, the author of the articles was Rev. John Thomas of Merthyr, see WCAM, p. 44.
20 *Y Goleuad*, January 10, 1900; April 18, 1900; January 31, 1900; *Yr Haul*, November 15, 1902.

CHAPTER 4 REFERENCES

1 *The Awakening in Wales 1904-5*, p. 9.
2 Extracts from the Seth Joshua diaries are based on the original entries. NLW CMA General 17916. Other sources on Seth Joshua include T. Mardy Rees, *Seth Joshua and Frank Joshua*, and Howell Williams, *The Romance of the Forward Movement*, p. 148.
3 *Y Drysorfa;* issues from April, 1961, to December, 1963, give extracts from John Thickens' papers relating to Joseph Jenkins; see also CGD, chapter 3.
4 DD, p. 393.

CHAPTER 5 REFERENCES

1 RRW, iii, p. 31, 29-30.
2 DMPW, pp. 119-20; DMPE, pp. 94, 95.
3 RRW, iii, p. 30.
4 J. J. Morgan, *The '59 Revival in Wales*, 1909, p. 11.
5 Edward Morgan, *The Life and Times of Howell Harris*, 1852, p. 10.
6 RRW, iii, p. 30.
7 RRW, iii, p. 30.
8 DMPW, pp. 160-1; DMPE, pp. 124-5; RRW, iii, p. 31.

9 DMPW, p. 196; DMPE, p. 160.
10 J. J. Morgan, *Cofiant Evan Phillips*, 1930, p. 332.
11 DMPW, p. 181; DMPE, p. 139.
12 DMPW, pp. 184-5; DMPE, p. 142.
13 DMPW, pp. 193-4; DMPE, pp. 157-8.
14 DMPW, p. 200; DMPE, p. 154.

CHAPTER 6 REFERENCES

1 DMPW, pp. 223-5; DMPE, pp. 166-8.
2 DMPW, pp. 215-16.
3 W. T. Stead, *The Revival in the West*, n.d., pp. 47-8, quoting *South Wales Daily News*, November 19th, 1904. See also DMPW, pp. 216-17.
4 W. T. Stead, *op. cit.*, p. 48.
5 DMPW, pp. 212-14.
6 DMPW, p. 218.
7 *op. cit.*, p. 45.
8 DMPW, p. 292; DMPE, p. 224.
9 DMPW, p. 303; DMPE, p. 234.
10 DMPW, pp. 260, 289; DMPE, 194, 221.
11 DD, p. 398.
12 DMPW, p. 304; DMPE, p. 235.
13 DMPW, p. 288; DMPE, p. 220.
14 DMPW, p. 314; DMPE, p. 237.
15 DMPW, p. 261; DMPE, pp. 194-5.
16 DMPW, p. 289; DMPE, p. 221.
17 DMPW, p. 293; DMPE, p. 223.
18 DMPW, pp. 303-04; DMPE, pp. 234-5.
19 DMPW, p. 263; DMPE, pp. 195-6.
20 DMPW, p. 314; DMPE, pp. 237-8.
21 DMPW, p. 292; DMPE, p. 223.
22 DMPW, pp. 265-6, 304; DMPE, pp. 197, 235; DD, pp. 57-8.
23 DMPW, p. 266; DMPE, p. 198.
24 DMPW, pp. 267-8; DMPE, p. 199.
25 DMPW, p. 314; DMPE, p. 238.
26 DMPW, p. 305; DMPE, pp. 235-6.
27 *ibid.*
28 DMPW, p. 294; DMPE, p. 225.
29 DMPW, p. 288; DMPE, p. 220.
30 DMPW, p. 313; DMPE, pp. 236, 237.
31 DMPW, p. 296; DMPE, pp. 227-8.
32 DD, p. 59.
33 DMPW, p. 275; DMPE, p. 206.
34 DD, p. 61.
35 DMPW, pp. 275-6; DMPE, p. 207.
36 DD, p. 59.
37 Quoted in Mary N. Garrard, *op. cit.* (1947), p. 224.

THE WELSH REVIVAL OF 1904

DMPW, pp. 277-8, 300, 307; DMPE, pp. 208, 231-2, 240; DD, p. 60.
DMPW, pp. 314-15.
DMPW, p. 307; DMPE, pp. 239-40.
DMPW, p. 317; DMPE, p. 244.
RRW, i, pp. 4, 5.
DMPW, p. 317; DMPE, p. 244.
DMPW, pp. 280-2; DMPE, pp. 213-14.
DMPW, p. 318; DMPE, p. 245.
RRW, i, p. 2.
DMPW, pp. 284-6; DMPE, pp. 217-18.
DMPW, pp. 299, 302; DMPE, pp. 230, 233.
DMPW, pp. 300, 307; DMPE, pp. 232, 240.
DMPW, pp. 279-80; DMPE, pp. 212-13.
DMPW, p. 307; DMPE, p. 240.
DMPW, p. 300; DMPE, p. 232.
DMPW, p. 283; DMPE, pp. 215-16.

CHAPTER 7 REFERENCES

DD, p. 393; DMPW, p. 196.
DMPW, p. 299; DMPE, p. 230.
DMPW, pp. 290, 299; DMPE, pp. 221, 230.
DMPW, p. 302; DMPE, p. 233; DD, p. 396.
DMPW, p. 301; DMPE, pp. 232-3.
DMPW, pp. 298, 299; DMPE, pp. 229, 230.
DD, pp. 154, 155.
DD, pp. 155, 156.
Y Drysorfa, 1963, p. 259.
Y Drysorfa, 1905, pp. 250-2.
DD, pp. 124-8.
DD, p. 125; NLW CMA General 17916; CGD, p. 89.
DD, p. 128.
Y Dysgedydd, 1952, p. 179.
O Gopa Bryn Nebo (From the top of Mount Nebo), 1967, p. 70. These reminiscences originally appeared in Y Goleuad during 1955. His experiences of the revival are given on pp. 61-83.
O Gopa Bryn Nebo, p. 66.
RRW, i, p. 31.
CGD, pp. 89-91; Robert Ellis, Living Echoes of the Welsh Revival, n.d., p. 94.
DD, p. 173.
JVM, p. 116.
Y Goleuad, February 5, 1904.
DMPW, pp. 306, 310; DMPE, p. 243; DD, pp. 135, 187; Y Drysorfa, 1905, p. 505.
Yr Herald Cymraeg, January 17, 1905, 'Y Diwygiad'.

25 *ibid*, May 2, 1905, 'Stratford, Llundain'.
26 Hugh Ellis, *Hanes Methodistiaeth Gorllewin Meirionydd*, vol. iii, 1928, p. 339; Hugh Owen, *Hanes Methodistiaeth Môn*, 1937, p. 378; Hugh Jones, *Hanes Wesleyaeth Gymreig*, vol. iii, 1912, p. 999.
27 *Caernarvon and Denbigh Herald*, 16 December, 1904, 'The Religious Revival'.
28 DD, p. 146.
29 *Caernarvon and Denbigh Herald*, 2 December, 1904, 'The Religious Revival'.
30 DD, pp. 166, 178, 216.
31 DD, pp. 217, 218.
32 DD, pp. 219-20.
33 *Yr Herald Cymraeg*, February 28, 1905, 'Y Diwygiad'.
34 RRW, vi, p. 29.
35 WCAM, pp. 124-5; *cf* CGD, p. 68.
36 Henry Johnson, *Stories of Great Revivals*, 1906, p. 356, quoting the *South Wales Daily News*.
37 DD, p. 175; *Caernarvon and Denbigh Herald*, 2 December, 1904.
38 *Caernarvon and Denbigh Herald*, 16 December, 1904.
39 RRW, iii, p. 17; CGD, p. 80; *Yr Herald Cymraeg*, January 3, 1905, 'Y Diwygiad'.
40 *Yr Herald Cymraeg*, December 27, 1904.
41 *ibid*, January 10, 1905.
42 *ibid*, January 17, 31, 1905; *Caernarvon and Denbigh Herald*, January 13, February 10, 1905.
43 *Yr Herald Cymraeg*, January 24, 1905.
44 *ibid*, December 20, 1904; January 31, 1905.
45 *Y Goleuad*, June 9, 1905.
46 Hugh Ellis, *op. cit.*, pp. 310-11.
47 *ibid*, pp. 244, 120, 231, 311.
48 DD, pp. 210-12; CGD, pp. 70-1, 77-8, *cf*. A. T. Fryer, *Proceedings of the Society of Psychical Research*, December, 1905, 'Psychological Aspects of the Welsh Revival'.
49 Hugh Ellis, *op. cit.*, p. 313.
50 WCAM, p. 103; DD, p. 346.
51 *Rhos Herald*, June 25, 1904.
52 *Rhos Herald*, November 26, 1904; DD, pp. 347-8.
53 *Y Goleuad*, November 25, 1904.
54 DD, pp. 350-3; WCAM, p. 104.
55 DD, pp. 356-7.
56 WCAM, pp. 112, 113.
57 DD, p. 353.

CHAPTER 8 REFERENCES

1 DMPE, p. 305.
2 RRW, iv. p. 7.

[3] DMPE, p. 2; DMPW, preface.
[4] RRW, iii. pp. 13-14.
[5] RRW, iv. p. 5.
[6] DMPE, p. 256.
[7] RRW, i. p. 11.
[8] RRW, i. p. 25.
[9] RRW, i. p. 22.
[10] RRW, i. p. 30.
[11] RRW, i. p. 16.
[12] DMPE, p. 305.
[13] RRW, i. p. 26; ii. p. 22, 3.
[14] DMPE, pp. 302-03.
[15] RRW, ii. p. 23.
[16] RRW, ii. pp. 16-18.
[17] RRW, ii. p. 10.
[18] DMPE, p. 340; DMPW, p. 333.
[19] RRW, iii. p. 31.
[20] RRW, ii. pp. 28-9.
[21] DMPE, p. 344.
[22] DMPE, pp. 353-4; DMPW, p. 334.
[23] JVM, pp. 143-5.
[24] RRW, iv. p. 3.
[25] *Yr Herald Cymraeg*, February 7, 1905, 'Y Diwygiad'.
[26] F. J. A. Hort, *The Ante-Nicene Fathers*, 1895, p. 100.
[27] See Philip Schaff, *History of the Christian Church* (Ante-Nicene Christianity), vol. ii, 1889, pp. 417-27.
[28] *ibid.*, p. 419.
[29] Tom Beynon, *Howell Harris's Visits to Pembrokeshire*, 1966, p. 182; *cf.* Geoffrey F. Nuttall, *Howel Harris 1714-1773*, 1965, pp. 51-3.
[30] Eifion Evans, *op. cit.*, 2nd Ed. pp. 60-61.
[31] RRW, iv. pp. 10, 12, 18, 22
[32] WCAM, p. 148.
[33] Quoted in CGD, p. 81.
[34] RRW, iv. p. 4.
[35] RRW, iv. pp. 26, 30-32.
[36] *Y Goleuad*, March 17, 1905.
[37] *Journal*, 7 July, 1739.
[38] *Fy Mhererindod Ysbrydol* (My Spiritual Pilgrimage), 1938, pp. 74-5.
[39] DMPE, p. 485; DMPW, p. 391.
[40] Mrs. Penn-Lewis in collaboration with Evan Roberts, *War on the Saints*, 1912, p. 283.
[41] RRW, v. pp. 19, 20.
[42] NLW CMA George Davies MS 2, 22 and 26 January, 1905.
[43] RRW, vi. p. 29.
[44] DMPE, p. 380.
[45] John Hughes Morris, *Hanes Methodistiaeth Liverpool*, vol. i. 1929, p. 266.

46 RRW, vi. pp. 4, 18.
47 RRW, vi. pp. 11, 6, 21.
48 RRW, vi. pp. 15, 20.
49 *Darluniadur Eglwys Rydd y Cymry 1901-1906*, 1906 (Pictorial Souvenir of the Free Church of the Welsh).
50 RRW, vi. p. 23.
51 RRW, vi. pp. 24, 26.
52 The *Liverpool Daily Post and Mercury*, 13 April, 1905.
53 DMPE, pp. 402-3.
54 *War on the Saints*, p. 45.
55 RRW, vi. p. 27.
56 Mrs. Penn-Lewis, *The Awakening in Wales (1904-1905)*, pp. 36, 37.
57 DMPE, pp. 404, 405.
58 Hugh Owen, *Braslun o Hanes M. C. Môn, (1880-1935)*, 1937, pp. 146, 221, 245, 380.
59 DMPE, p. 490.
60 *The British Weekly* (Special Supplement), 7 December, 1905.

CHAPTER 9 REFERENCES

1 DD, p. 317; *cf.* NLW CMA General 15051, and David O. Hughes, *Canrif o Hanes . . .* (1909), pp. 68-81; DD, p. 227.
2 DD, pp. 275-7.
3 Calvinistic Methodist *Year Book for 1936*, p. 147; *Bathafarn*, xv, 22; R. Tudur Jones, *op. cit.*, p. 237; cf JVM, p. 249.
4 DMPE, p. 451.
5 *Yr Herald Cymraeg*, January 17, 1905, 'Y Diwygiad'.
6 *ibid*, February 7, 1905.
7 *ibid*, March 28, 1905.
8 *The Christian*, 30 November, 1905.
9 *ibid*, 29 June; 7 September, 1905.
10 WCAM, pp. 185-6.
11 *Missionary Review of the World*, 1905, p. 878; 1906, p. 566.
12 *The Christian*, 3 August, 1905.
13 *Y Goleuad*, March 3, 1905; *Yr Herald Cymraeg*, February 28, 1905.
14 Western edition, 22 February, 1905.
15 *Alliance Weekly*, 1906, pp. 177, 222.
16 *Missionary Review of the World*, 1905, p. 229.
17 *Yr Herald Cymraeg*, January 24, 1905.
18 Reuben Saillens, *The Soul of France*, p. 211 (quoted in D. D. Williams, *Llawlyfr Hanes Cyfundeb y Methodistiaid Calfinaidd*, n.d., p. 249, footnote).
19 CGD, p. 74. *Un Mouvement Mystique Contemporain; le Reveil Religieux du Pays de Galles (1904-1905)*, par J. Rogues de Fursac, Paris, 1907.
20 *ibid*, p. 75. *Le Reveil au Pays de Galles*, par Henri Bois, Toulouse, (1906-07).

21 Michael Harper, *As at the Beginning*, 1966, p. 30.
22 Nils Bloch-Hoell, *The Pentecostal Movement*, 1964, p. 201, note 188. For Barratt see pp. 178-9.
23 *ibid*, p. 201, note 189, referring to Birger Hall, *Vækkelsen i Wales. En beretning efter engelske kilder.*
24 *Missionary Review of the World*, 1906, pp. 310, 458; cf. *The Christian*, 14 December, 1905.
25 *The Christian*, 19 January, 1905.
26 *Den Indremissionens Historie*, Copenhagen, 1912, p. 362; *Indre Missions Tidende*, Copenhagen, 1906, p. 331.
27 P. Scharpff, *Geschichte der Evangelisation*, Giesen, 1964, pp. 279-81.
28 *The Christian*, 21 September, 1905.
29 *ibid*, 10 August; 2 November, 1905; *Missionary Review of the World*, 1905, p. 309.
30 *Missionary Review of the World*, 1906, pp. 308, 405.
31 *Methodist Churchman*, Cape Town, 4 July; 8 August, 1905; *De Kerkbode*, Cape Town, 3, 24 August; 12 October, 1905; *De Christelijke Strever*, Cape Town, September, 1905.
32 *Australian Christian World*, 1905 issues.
33 *The Outlook*, Dunedin, 21 January; 30 September; 7 October, 1905; *The Christian*, 23 November, 1905.
34 D. MacGillivray, *A Century of Protestant Missions in China*, Shanghai, 1907, p. 211; *Missionary Review of the World*, 1905, p. 36.
35 *China's Millions*, 1906, p. 141; 1907, p. 14.
36 A. W. Wasson, *Church Growth in Korea*, New York, 1934, pp. 31-32.
37 Stephen Neill, *Christian Missions*, 1964, p. 343.
38 *Missionary Review of the World*, 1905, pp. 474-5; 555, ff; 955.
39 L. G. Paik, *The History of Protestant Missions in Korea 1832-1910*, Pyeng Yang, 1929, p. 357.
40 J. Pengwern Jones, *India Awake! Thy King Has Come*, Second edition, August, 1905, p. 22. The first and shorter edition had appeared in May, 1905.
41 Mrs. John Roberts, *Y Diwygiad ar Fryniau Khassia* (1907), p. 5.
42 *ibid*, pp. 6-7.
43 J. Pengwern Jones, *op. cit.*, p. 23.
44 *ibid*, pp. 28-9.
45 *op. cit.*, p. 52.
46 J. Pengwern Jones, *op cit.*, p. 39.
47 *ibid*, pp. 39-40.
48 *ibid*, p. 58.
49 Mrs. John Roberts, *op. cit.*, p. 46.
50 Frederick Henke, *American Journal of Theology*, vol. xiii (1909), pp. 193, ff; 'The Gift of Tongues and Related Phenomena of the Present Day'.
51 J. Pengwern Jones, *op. cit.*, pp. 56-7.

[52] *ibid*, p. 49.
[53] Mrs. John Roberts, *op. cit.*, p. 109.
[54] CGD, pp. 107, 104.
[55] J. A. Baker, *Contending the Grade*, Asheville, 1947, pp. 103, ff; *cf.*, Baker's letter of 18 April, 1906, in the Archives of American Baptist Foreign Mission at Valley Forge.
[56] Frank Houghton, *Amy Carmichael of Dohnavur*, 1955, pp. 146-8.
[57] Nicol MacNicol, *Pandita Ramabai*, Calcutta, 1926, pp. 117, 118; *Missionary Review of the World*, 1906, p. 552; H. S. Dyer, *Revival in India*, 1907, pp. 44, 55; *idem, Pandita Ramabai*, n.d., p. 11.
[58] *Alliance Weekly*, New York, 1907, p. 234.

CHAPTER 10 REFERENCES

[1] Hugh Owen, *op. cit.*, p. 49.
[2] *ibid*, p. 246.
[3] JVM, p. 247.
[4] *Seren Gomer*, March, 1905, p. 63.
[5] DMPE, p. 275.
[6] CGD, p. 73.
[7] DMPE, p. 330; RRW, i, pp. 29, 28.
[8] RRW, i, pp. 13, 29.
[9] DMPE, p. 337; RRW, ii, pp. 11-12; iii, pp. 19-20.
[10] DMPE, pp. 277-82.
[11] *The Revival in the West*, n.d., pp. 30, 34.
[12] 2 February, 1905, 'The Heart of the Revival'.
[13] January, 1905, p. 32.
[14] March, 1905, p. 63.
[15] January, 1905, p. 27; and July, 1905, pp. 159-60, respectively.
[16] JVM, p. 262.
[17] *op. cit.*, p. 49.
[18] *Yr Eurgrawn Wesleyaidd*, February, 1905, p. 66.
[19] Reprinted 1950, p. 28.
[20] *Caernarvon and Denbigh Herald*, 16 December, 1904, 'The Religious Revival'.
[21] Pp. 124, 129. Reports of the 1905 Keswick by J. B. Figgis, A. T. Pierson, and E. H. Hopkins appeared in *The Life of Faith*, August 16, 23, 30, 1905, and were reprinted in R. B. Jones, *Rent Heavens*, pp. 93-108.
[22] See Kathleen Heasman, *Evangelicals in Action*, 1962.
[23] Jn. 19 : 26; Gal. 4 : 4; Eph. 5 : 25; 1 Tim. 2 : 9; I Cor. 11 : 5; Acts 18 : 24-26.
[24] 1 Cor. 14 : 34; 1 Tim. 2 : 12.
[25] Gal. 3 : 28; 1 Pet. 3 : 7.
[26] 1 Pet. 3 : 1-6.

CHAPTER 11 REFERENCES

1 DMPE, p. 448.
2 DMPE, p. 453.
3 *Yr Herald Cymraeg*, March 27, 1906, 'Mr. Evan Roberts a'r esgob merthyredig'.
4 Mary N. Garrard, *op. cit.*, pp. 230-1.
5 *Yr Herald Cymraeg*, April 24, 1906, 'Mr. Evans Roberts ym Mangor'.
6 DMPE, p. 493; DMPW, p. 398. Jessie Penn-Lewis had published *The Cross of Calvary and its Message* in 1903 and a second edition was to appear in October, 1906.
7 DMPE, p. 454.
8 *The British Weekly*, 27 February, 1930.
9 *Western Mail*, 23 September, 1932.
10 *Blwyddiadur y Methodistiaid Calfinaidd am y flwyddyn 1911*, p. 99.
11 *South Wales News*, 25 January, 1927; 23 January, 1928.
12 *South Wales Daily Post*, 1 November, 1928, 'Evan Roberts at Loughor'.
13 *British Weekly*, 27 February, 1930; *Western Mail*, 7 June, 1930.
14 Calvinistic Methodist *Year Book for 1931*, pp. 151-2.
15 *Daily News and Chronicle* (Manchester Edition), 12 June, 1930, 'The influence of Evan Roberts'.
16 *Welsh Gazette*, 26 June, 1930; *Western Mail*, 30 June, 1930.
17 *British Weekly*, 21 August, 1930, 'Mr. Evan Roberts'.
18 *The Christian*, 28 August, 1930, 'Mr. Evan Roberts at Eisteddfod'.
19 *British Weekly*, 15 October, 1931, 'Mr. Evan Roberts'.
20 CGD, p. 118.
21 *Fy Mhererindod Ysbrydol*, p. 85.
22 WCAM, p. 209.
23 J. Pengwern Jones, *op. cit.*, p. 44.
24 J. Henry Williams, *Ar Ei Ben bo'r Goron*. A second edition in 1906 included a further two chapters, one on prayer and the other on 'Keswick, its history and teaching'.
25 *op. cit.*, p. 237.
26 David Williams, *A History of Modern Wales*, 1951, p. 266.
27 D. Eifion Evans, *Journal of the Historical Society of the Church in Wales*, vol. vii, No. 12 (1957), p. 95.
28 John Hughes, *Yr Ail Ganrif*, 1912, p. 19.
29 *Torri'r Rhaffau* (Cutting the ropes), 1925, pp. 13, 12, 14. The articles appeared originally in *Y Goleuad* under the same title, January 7, 14, 1925, and correspondence on the issue continued until March.
30 *O Gopa Bryn Nebo*, p. 97.
31 Pp. 284, 285.
32 Pp. 214, 300.
33 WCAM, pp. 158-9.
34 RRW, iv, p. 19.

[35] See Michael Harper, *op. cit.*, 1966, pp. 27, 28, 37; John Thomas Nichol, *Pentecostalism*, 1966, pp. 34, 58.

[36] *News Chronicle* (Welsh Edition), 20 October, 1947.

[37] Ernest C. W. Boulton, *George Jeffreys, A Ministry of the Miraculous,* c. 1928, pp. 12, 13, 20, ff.

[38] Thomas Napier Turnbull, *Brothers in Arms* (1963), pp. 33-4.

[39] *The Prophetical Ministry (or The Voice Gifts) in the Church,* (1931), pp. 98-99.

[40] *War on the Saints,* pp. 294-5; *cf.* p. 285.

[41] *The Pentecostal Movement,* 1949, p. 6, quoted in John Thomas Nichol, *op. cit.,* pp. 7, 40-1.

[42] Donald Gee, *op. cit.,* p. 88.

[43] T. B. Barratt, *Word and Work,* vol. xxxiii (April 1911), pp. 103, f, 'An urgent plea for charity and unity'.

[44] George Griffiths, *What God Hath Wrought,* 1962, p. 4.

[45] *op. cit.,* p. 58.

Index

Other books by Dr Eifion Evans published by the Evangelical Press of Wales:

REVIVAL COMES TO WALES

A moving and thrilling account of the mighty working of God the Holy Spirit in Wales at the time of the 1859 Revival.

TWO WELSH REVIVALISTS

The fascinating stories of Humphrey Jones and Dafydd Morgan, the two prominent leaders during the 1859 Revival in Wales.

REVIVALS: THEIR RISE, PROGRESS AND ACHIEVEMENTS

A general survey of revivals and their characteristics, concentrating especially on those of the eighteenth century.

Further titles from the Evangelical Press of Wales on the subject of revival:

REVIVAL AND ITS FRUIT
by Emyr Roberts & R. Geraint Gruffydd

Studies on the nature of revival and the phenomena associated with it.

HOWELL HARRIS AND THE DAWN OF REVIVAL
by Richard Bennett; introduction by D. Martyn Lloyd-Jones

Formerly published under the title *The Early Life of Howell Harris*, this book is an invaluable study of the early spiritual life of Howell Harris and the beginnings of the Great Awakening of the eighteenth century in Wales.

'EXCUSE ME, MR DAVIES — HALLELUJAH!'
by Geraint D. Fielder; foreword by Lady Catherwood

The absorbing story of evangelical student witness in Wales in the twentieth century, a story which includes periods of quite remarkable spiritual blessing.

Further titles from the Evangelical Press of Wales

MARTYN LLOYD-JONES:
THE MAN AND HIS BOOKS
by Frederick & Elizabeth Catherwood

A fascinating personal account of 'the Doctor' by his daughter and son-in-law.

WHY DOES GOD ALLOW WAR?
by D. Martyn Lloyd-Jones

Biblical teaching on how Christians should face evil and suffering.

OUT OF THE DEPTHS
by D. Martyn Lloyd-Jones

An exposition of Psalm 51 which deals with the problem of human failure and guilt and the divine remedy of repentance.

CHRISTIAN HYMNS
edited by Paul E.G. Cook and Graham Harrison

A comprehensive selection of 901 hymns highlighting both the objective and subjective aspects of the Christian faith, and including 80 metrical psalms and paraphrases. Music edition and a variety of words editions.

CHRISTIAN HYMN-WRITERS
by Elsie Houghton

A collection of brief biographies of some of the great hymn-writers (288 pages).

Books on contemporary issues published by the Evangelical Press of Wales:

SOCIAL ISSUES AND THE LOCAL CHURCH
Ian Shaw (editor)

Among the subjects covered by this work are: the Christian and the state, the Christian concern for education, the role of women in the church, social welfare and the local church, and mission in today's world.

CHRISTIAN FAMILY MATTERS
Ian Shaw (editor); foreword by Sir Frederick Catherwood

Here is clear biblical teaching by experienced contributors on marriage, parenthood, childhood and adolescence, the handicapped child, fostering and adoption, divorce, abortion and family planning, and the care of the elderly.

THE CHRISTIAN, THE CHURCH AND DAILY WORK
Gerallt Wyn Davies

In this little book the author looks at biblical teaching about work, compares it with society's attitudes, and outlines what individual Christians and the church could do to be of effective help in alleviating the great social problem of unemployment.

These publications are available from your local Christian bookshop, or in case of difficulty, from the publishers, Evangelical Press of Wales, Bryntirion, Bridgend, Mid Glamorgan CF31 4DX, Wales (postage extra). Catalogues giving full details of all publications, in English and in Welsh, are also available from the same address.